THE INFINITE TAPESTRY
A MASTERPIECE OF THEOLOGY, PHILOSOPHY, AND COSMOLOGY

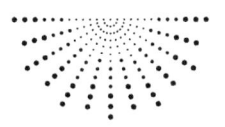

OMAR HAN

Copyright © 2025 by Omar Han

All rights reserved.

No part of this book may be reproduced in any form or by any electronic or mechanical means, including information storage and retrieval systems, without written permission from the author, except for the use of brief quotations in a book review.

PREFACE

In the beginning, there was a stirring—a silent, inexorable call from the depths of existence that beckoned the human spirit to seek out truth, beauty, and meaning. This work, *The Infinite Tapestry: A Masterpiece of Theology, Philosophy, and Cosmology*, is born of that call. It is the culmination of countless hours of reflection, debate, and exploration, a testament to the unquenchable human thirst for understanding the mysteries of the universe.

The journey that unfolds within these pages is not one of dry, abstract theorizing; it is a vibrant expedition into the heart of existence. Inspired by the luminous insights of al-Razi—a towering figure in Islamic thought who dared to challenge established paradigms and bridge the realms of revelation and reason—this magnum opus endeavors to weave together the strands of theology, philosophy, Qur'anic exegesis, and cosmology into a coherent and compelling narrative. It is a work that seeks not merely to answer questions, but to illuminate the very questions themselves, inviting the reader to participate in a dialogue that spans time, culture, and the very fabric of reality.

At its core, this book is an invitation. It invites scholars, seekers, and the curious alike to journey beyond the superficial and to explore the depths of human experience. Here, we encounter a cosmos that is not a barren void or a chaotic mishmash of random events, but a meticulously ordered design—an endless tapestry where every thread is interwoven with purpose, every moment a reflection of divine wisdom. From the intricate workings of the natural world to the lofty realms of the soul, the ideas presented herein are meant to challenge our conventional perceptions and inspire us to reimagine the limits of what we know.

This work is dedicated to those who believe that the search for truth is a lifelong endeavor. It is for the ones who look beyond the immediate, who dare to question the status quo, and who understand that true wisdom is found not in the certainty of answers but in the continual pursuit of understanding. In these pages, you will find not only the intellectual legacy of past masters but also a call to modern inquiry—a challenge to harmonize empirical insight with spiritual revelation, to blend the clarity of reason with the mystery of the divine.

As you turn these pages, may you feel the quiet power of contemplation and the stirring of your own inner voice. May this book serve as both a map and a mirror, guiding you toward new horizons of thought while reflecting the eternal quest that lies at the heart of every human being. For in the grand tapestry of existence, every soul is both a seeker and a weaver, contributing its own unique pattern to the infinite design.

Welcome to *The Infinite Tapestry*. May your journey through its chapters be as transformative and boundless as the universe it seeks to unveil.

PROLOGUE

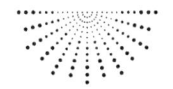

IN THE QUIET RECESSES OF A TIMELESS UNIVERSE, WHERE THE boundaries between the seen and the unseen dissolve into a single, intricate tapestry of mystery and meaning, there emerges a vision—a vision of the cosmos not as a cold, mechanical construct, but as a living, breathing manifestation of divine wisdom. *The Infinite Tapestry: A Masterpiece of Theology, Philosophy, and Cosmology* invites us on a journey that spans the breadth of human inquiry and touches upon the very essence of existence. In these pages, under the evocative pseudonym of Omar Han, the reader is called to explore a realm where reason and revelation, tradition and innovation, the empirical and the mystical, intertwine in a dance as ancient as time itself.

THIS WORK IS BORN from the perennial quest to understand the ultimate nature of reality—a quest that has driven scholars, mystics, and seekers for millennia. Here, the reader encounters a synthesis of ideas that transcends the limitations of conventional discourse. The author draws on the illustrious legacy of Islamic thought, weaving together the profound insights of theologians, philosophers, and scientists who dared to question, to dream, and to imagine a universe where every particle and every thought is imbued with purpose. In this grand narrative, the cosmos is not merely a backdrop for human endeavors; it is an eloquent testament to the creative power of the Divine.

Within these chapters, one will discover an exploration of cosmic order and human destiny—a detailed account of the mechanisms that govern the heavens and the intricate dance of creation that pulses at the heart of all things. The text delves into the nature of knowledge, the delicate balance between good and evil, and the eternal interplay of fate and free will. It challenges the reader to reconsider the familiar, urging us to look beyond the superficial layers of everyday life and to glimpse the profound truths that lie beneath.

At its core, *The Infinite Tapestry* is a call to awaken—to recognize that every moment, every choice, every breath is part of a vast, interwoven design that reflects both the infinite grandeur of the cosmos and the intimate intricacies of the human soul. It is an invitation to embrace the complexities of faith and reason, to see the beauty in paradox, and to find solace in the knowledge that, although our understanding may be finite, our capacity for wonder and discovery is boundless.

This prologue, then, serves as the threshold to a journey of both intellectual and spiritual exploration. It sets the stage for a series of inquiries into the most profound questions of existence: the nature of truth and certainty, the mysterious interplay of time and space, and the ultimate destiny of the soul. As you embark on this voyage through the pages that follow, may you find not only answers but also new questions—each a stepping stone toward a deeper, more nuanced understanding of the eternal tapestry that binds us all.

WELCOME to a world where the sacred and the rational converge, where the echo of ancient wisdom meets the pulse of modern inquiry, and where every chapter is a tribute to the unending pursuit of truth.

1
LIFE AND INTELLECTUAL CONTEXT

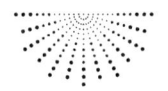

IN THIS OPENING CHAPTER, WE EMBARK ON A JOURNEY INTO the life and mind of Fakhr al-Din al-Razi, whose luminous intellect and restless inquiry continue to inspire scholars centuries beyond his time. His biography, set against the rich tapestry of 12th-century intellectual ferment, provides a foundation for understanding not only his own transformative ideas but also the broader currents that shaped Islamic thought. In what follows, we delve into the contours of his life, the vibrant milieu in which he lived, and the profound legacy of his writings.

BIOGRAPHY OF AL-RAZI

BORN into modest circumstances in the ancient city of Ray, al-Razi—formally known as Abu Bakr Muhammad ibn Zakariyya al-Razi—emerged as one of the foremost polymaths of his age. From an early period, his insatiable curiosity led him to traverse diverse fields of knowledge: medicine, philosophy, theology, and the natural sciences. His life, marked by an ardent commitment to reason and revelation, reflects a relentless quest for truth that would become his hallmark.

AL-RAZI'S formative years were steeped in the traditions of rigorous scholarship. As a young man, he absorbed not only the doctrinal teachings of his religious community but also the vibrant, eclectic discourses that permeated the scholarly circles of his region. His education was not confined to the religious sciences; he was equally versed in the rational sciences of logic, mathematics, and natural philosophy. This synthesis of diverse disciplines—integrating the spiritual with the empirical—became a defining characteristic of his later work. Over time, his reputation grew, attracting disciples and admirers who sought to glimpse the method behind his intricate analyses of existence and the cosmos.

THE COURSE of al-Razi's life was punctuated by personal trials and triumphs, each leaving an indelible mark on his thought. Amid the political and cultural turbulence of his time, he maintained an unwavering commitment to intellectual integrity. His writings, which spanned treatises on ethics, cosmology, and metaphysics, reveal not only a brilliant mind but also a compassionate spirit deeply concerned with the human condition. His biography thus serves as both an inspiring narrative of individual achievement and a mirror reflecting the broader challenges and aspirations of a world in transformation.

THE INTELLECTUAL MILIEU of the 12th Century

. . .

THE 12TH CENTURY in the Islamic world was a period of extraordinary intellectual vitality. It was an era where reason and revelation engaged in a dynamic dialogue—a dialogue that would eventually lead to profound advancements in theology, philosophy, and the natural sciences. The cultural crossroads at which al-Razi found himself was characterized by a robust exchange of ideas between Greek, Persian, and Indian traditions, all filtered through the prism of Islamic thought.

THIS PERIOD WITNESSED the flourishing of institutions of learning, where scholars debated and refined concepts that ranged from the metaphysical to the empirical. The legacy of earlier thinkers, such as al-Farabi and Avicenna, provided a rich intellectual substrate that al-Razi both inherited and transcended. The atmosphere was one of rigorous debate, where established doctrines were constantly challenged by innovative perspectives. In such a climate, al-Razi's insistence on questioning received wisdom—coupled with his ability to reconcile contradictory ideas—allowed him to chart new intellectual territories.

MOREOVER, the sociopolitical context of the time cannot be underestimated. The period was marked by the expansion of trade, the spread of ideas through a network of scholars, and the patronage of learning by enlightened rulers. These factors converged to create a milieu in which intellectual inquiry was not only possible but also vigorously encouraged. The debates on theology, philosophy, and science were not confined to cloisters or courts but resonated across the broader society, influencing art, literature, and even everyday life. It is within this rich tapestry of exchange and innovation that al-Razi's thought took root, flourishing amid both convergence and divergence of ideas.

AL-RAZI'S MAJOR Works and Their Impact

THE LITERARY OUTPUT of al-Razi is as vast and intricate as the tapestry of ideas he wove throughout his life. His major works span a spectrum of disciplines, each piece reflecting a rigorous methodology that marries reason with divine insight. Among these, his treatises on theology and philosophy stand as monumental achievements, offering penetrating analyses of the nature of God, the structure of the universe, and the limits of human understanding.

ONE OF HIS most celebrated contributions lies in his systematic approach to reconciling faith with rational inquiry. In his theological works, al-Razi sought to demystify the divine, stripping away anthropomorphic conceptions to reveal a transcendent and omnipotent God. His critical stance towards traditional Aristotelian cosmology, in favor of more innovative models that anticipated later multiverse theories, signaled a paradigm shift in the understanding of the cosmos. Through works that examined the infinite nature of the universe and the plurality of worlds, he not only challenged established dogmas but also opened new vistas for both scientific and metaphysical exploration.

THE IMPACT of al-Razi's scholarship extended well beyond the confines of academic debate. His writings influenced successive generations of theologians, philosophers, and scientists, both within the Islamic world and in the Latin

West. By engaging with the pressing questions of his time—questions of existence, morality, and the nature of reality—he laid the groundwork for later intellectual revolutions. His insistence on critical inquiry and the harmonious coexistence of faith and reason resonated deeply, fostering an intellectual legacy that continues to shape contemporary discourse.

In summary, al-Razi's major works serve as a testament to the enduring power of a mind that dared to question and to synthesize disparate strands of knowledge. His influence, evident in both his direct contributions and the subsequent evolution of intellectual thought, marks him as a true pioneer—a visionary who transformed the contours of medieval scholarship and left an indelible mark on the course of human thought.

Thus, the life and context of al-Razi present a multifaceted portrait of a scholar deeply engaged with the perennial questions of existence. His biography, interwoven with the rich intellectual tapestry of the 12th century, sets the stage for a journey into the profound realms of theology, philosophy, and cosmology. As we move forward in this work, we invite the reader to reflect on the legacy of a mind that forever altered the landscape of knowledge and to consider how his insights continue to illuminate the eternal quest for truth.

2
METHODOLOGY AND APPROACH

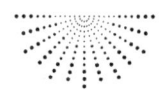

In this chapter, we explore the intricate methods that underpin al-Razi's intellectual legacy. His approach is not a mere collection of techniques but a coherent, evolving system that marries the spiritual with the rational. Central to his work is the synthesis of theology and philosophy, a marriage that allowed him to navigate the complex realms of divine mystery and empirical inquiry. Here, we examine the foundational elements of his method—his unique synthesis of disciplines, his innovative use of logic and dialectic, and his unwavering commitment to doubt and inquiry.

Al-Razi's Synthesis of Theology and Philosophy

Al-Razi's thought is marked by an ambitious and refreshing integration of theology with philosophy—a bold move at a time when these fields often found themselves at odds. He saw theology not as a static set of doctrines but as a dynamic process of understanding the divine, one that could be enriched by the insights of rational analysis. In his works, the spiritual and the logical are not isolated compartments but interwoven strands of the same tapestry.

HE ARGUED that the quest for divine truth could not be accomplished through blind adherence to tradition alone. Instead, it required the active engagement of the intellect—reason, speculation, and argument all played vital roles. This approach allowed him to address complex theological questions with the clarity and precision of a philosopher, while still acknowledging the mysteries inherent in the nature of God. His writings suggest that the divine is not distant and unapproachable but accessible through the careful and systematic use of reason. This groundbreaking synthesis laid the groundwork for later thinkers who would further bridge the gap between faith and rational thought.

THE RESULT IS a methodology that remains influential: one where theological assertions are constantly subjected to critical scrutiny, yet where philosophical inquiry is always imbued with a sense of reverence for the transcendent. Al-Razi's work demonstrates that faith and reason are not adversaries but complementary paths leading to a more profound understanding of existence. His synthesis invites readers to embrace complexity rather than settle for oversimplified answers, encouraging a lifelong pursuit of wisdom that values both certainty and mystery.

His Use of Logic and Dialectic

AT THE HEART of al-Razi's intellectual method lies a robust commitment to logic and dialectic. Logic, for him, was not merely a tool for constructing arguments—it was the language through which truth could be articulated and refined. He championed clear reasoning as a means of uncovering the principles that govern both the natural world and the realm of the divine.

AL-RAZI'S logical framework was rigorous yet flexible. He was well-versed in the classical traditions of Greek philosophy, yet he was unafraid to adapt and expand upon these foundations. By employing a dialectical method—whereby thesis and antithesis engage in a dynamic interplay—he sought to expose contradictions and resolve them through reasoned debate. This dialectic was not aimed at dismissing opposing views outright but at revealing the deeper truths that lay hidden within them. Each argument was a step towards refining a broader understanding, a process of perpetual revision and improvement.

IN HIS WRITINGS, you can observe the meticulous dissection of ideas. He often began with a series of definitions and propositions, carefully laying out the parameters of the discussion. From there, he would methodically examine each point, posing counterarguments and then reconciling them with his overall thesis. This method of analysis was not intended to reach a final, immutable conclusion but to engage the reader in an ongoing process of discovery. The interplay of logic and dialectic in his work reflects a deep belief in the power of reason to bridge the gap between the finite human mind and the infinite mysteries of the universe.

THIS APPROACH WAS radical in its time, challenging the notion that theological truths were beyond the reach of human reason. Instead, al-Razi argued that through disciplined argumentation and systematic inquiry, one could approach a more nuanced understanding of both the divine and the cosmos. His method underscores a commitment to clarity and precision, demanding that every claim be substantiated and every contradiction resolved. In doing so, he set a high standard for intellectual discourse—one that resonates with the principles of debate and inquiry still prized in scholarly pursuits today.

The Role of Doubt and Inquiry in His Thought

Perhaps one of the most striking aspects of al-Razi's methodology is his embrace of doubt as an essential component of the intellectual journey. Far from being a sign of weakness, doubt was, for him, the driving force behind genuine inquiry. It was the spark that ignited the pursuit of knowledge, urging both the thinker and the reader to question assumptions and probe deeper into the nature of reality.

Al-Razi maintained that doubt was not a precursor to nihilism but a critical step towards enlightenment. In his view, certainty is often the enemy of progress, as it can lead to complacency and the uncritical acceptance of established dogmas. Instead, he championed a rigorous skepticism—a disciplined doubt that demanded evidence and clear reasoning before any claim could be accepted as truth. This was not doubt for its own sake; rather, it was a methodological tool designed to refine understanding and eliminate errors.

. . .

The importance of inquiry in al-Razi's thought cannot be overstated. Every treatise he wrote was underpinned by a relentless questioning of both tradition and self. His writings reveal a mind that was unafraid to confront paradoxes, to wrestle with uncertainties, and to acknowledge the limitations of human understanding. This openness to questioning allowed him to navigate complex issues with a flexibility that was rare in his time. Rather than clinging to simplistic answers, he recognized that the journey toward knowledge is one of continual refinement—where each question leads to further questions, and every answer is but a stepping stone to greater understanding.

Al-Razi's method of inquiry also had a profoundly ethical dimension. It demanded intellectual humility—a recognition that no human, however learned, could claim complete mastery over the mysteries of existence. This humility was not an admission of defeat but a celebration of the infinite potential for growth and discovery. By placing doubt and inquiry at the center of his methodology, al-Razi not only advanced a powerful epistemological framework but also fostered an enduring spirit of curiosity that continues to inspire scholars across disciplines.

Conclusion

In synthesizing theology with philosophy, employing a rigorous logical framework, and embracing doubt as a vital tool of inquiry, al-Razi forged a methodology that remains as relevant today as it was revolutionary in his own time. His approach challenges us to rethink the boundaries between faith and reason, urging us to engage with the world through a lens that is both critically analytical and deeply reverent. Through his writings, al-Razi invites us to participate in a timeless dialogue—a conversation in which the pursuit of truth is an ever-evolving tapestry woven from threads of logic, reflection, and an insatiable quest for understanding.

As we continue our journey through this work, we will see how these methodological principles are not only theoretical constructs but are lived experiences that permeate every aspect of al-Razi's scholarship. His legacy is a testament to the transformative power of inquiry, a beacon for all who dare to question and to dream of a more enlightened future.

3
THE SOURCES OF HUMAN KNOWLEDGE

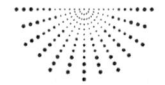

In this chapter, we embark on an expansive exploration of the diverse sources from which human beings derive knowledge. Drawing on al-Razi's incisive insights, we examine how knowledge is not a monolithic entity but a multifaceted tapestry woven from the threads of sensory experience, rational inquiry, divine revelation, and the systematic classification of the sciences. Al-Razi's perspective, as articulated in works like *Al-Matalib al-'Aliya*, reminds us that understanding the nature and limits of our cognitive faculties is the very foundation upon which any meaningful inquiry must rest.

Sense Perception and Its Limitations

Sense perception forms the initial point of contact between the human mind and the external world. It is through the senses—sight, sound, touch, taste, and smell—that we engage with our surroundings. Al-Razi, ever the empiricist in spirit, underscores that while sensory experience is indispensable, it is also inherently limited. The senses, by their very nature, provide only a partial and often deceptive representation of reality. They are susceptible to error, distortion, and the constraints of time and space.

CONSIDER, for instance, the phenomenon of optical illusions or the variability in auditory perception in different environments. Al-Razi observed that while our senses offer us the raw data of experience, they cannot capture the full essence of the objects they perceive. They are, in effect, the starting points—a necessary yet insufficient basis for comprehensive understanding. This recognition of sensory limitations compels the mind to seek further clarification through the instruments of reason and interpretation. The empirical data must be sifted, refined, and reinterpreted if it is to contribute to a deeper, more reliable body of knowledge.

MOREOVER, al-Razi was aware that the reliability of the senses can vary depending on the conditions under which they operate. The same sight that dazzles in bright light might obscure details in the dimness of dusk, and a sound may be misinterpreted in the chaos of a crowded environment. Thus, while sensory perception remains a vital source of knowledge, it is one that must be constantly calibrated against other measures of truth.

THE ROLE of Reason in Acquiring Knowledge

WHERE THE SENSES offer the raw and often ambiguous data of the world, reason serves as the refining fire that distills clarity and coherence from the chaos. For al-Razi, reason is not simply a tool among many; it is the guiding principle that enables humanity to transcend the immediate and often misleading impressions of sensory experience. Through rational reflection and logical analysis, the mind can integrate disparate pieces of evidence into a unified whole.

AL-RAZI'S COMMITMENT to the power of reason is evident in his rigorous method of argumentation. He advocated that the intellect, when properly exercised, is capable of discerning the underlying principles that govern both nature and metaphysical realities. In this light, reason functions as the mediator between the world of appearances and the deeper truths that lie beyond immediate perception. It allows for the systematic questioning of assumptions and the critical assessment of evidence. For al-Razi, the process of reasoning is iterative—each conclusion invites further questioning, and each doubt becomes a stepping stone toward a more refined understanding.

THIS RELIANCE on reason does not imply a cold, detached rationalism but rather a balanced engagement with the world—a synthesis of the empirical and the abstract. In his view, the human mind is endowed with the capacity to progress from the particular to the universal, from the sensory to the intellectual. The use of deductive and inductive methods, along with the dialectical process of resolving contradictions, forms the bedrock of his epistemological framework. Reason, in al-Razi's thought, is the bridge that connects the fleeting impressions of the senses with the enduring principles of truth.

REVELATION AS A SOURCE **of Knowledge**

. . .

WHILE SENSE PERCEPTION and reason are critical to the acquisition of knowledge, al-Razi did not confine the realm of understanding solely to the material or the rational. Revelation occupies a unique and exalted position in his epistemology. It is through divine revelation that human beings gain access to truths that transcend the limitations of both empirical observation and logical deduction.

REVELATION, as understood in the Islamic intellectual tradition, is the communication of divine wisdom through sacred texts and prophetic teachings. Al-Razi acknowledged that there exist dimensions of reality that remain forever beyond the grasp of reason alone. These are the mysteries of existence, the questions of purpose, and the nature of the divine—domains in which human intellect, no matter how powerful, must rely on the light of revelation to illuminate its path.

AL-RAZI'S APPROACH to revelation is nuanced. He was not content to accept divine pronouncements on blind faith alone; rather, he sought to understand and interpret these revelations through the lens of reason. In his writings, he often engages in a dialogue between the insights of revelation and the conclusions of philosophical inquiry. This interplay not only enriches the understanding of each but also ensures that divine wisdom is interpreted in a manner that is both intellectually robust and spiritually meaningful.

IN THIS CONTEXT, revelation complements reason. It offers insights that are otherwise inaccessible, imbuing the human quest for knowledge with a dimension of sacred profundity. The truths revealed are not arbitrary edicts but are imbued with a wisdom that aligns with the natural order and the rational structure of the universe. Thus, for al-Razi, revelation serves as an essential corrective to the shortcomings of the senses and the potential overreach of human reason, anchoring knowledge in a transcendent source of certainty.

THE CLASSIFICATION of Sciences (from Al-Matalib al-'Aliya)

AN ESSENTIAL CONTRIBUTION of al-Razi's thought is his systematic classification of the sciences, a project most vividly encapsulated in his work *Al-Matalib al-'Aliya*. In an era where knowledge was burgeoning in every conceivable field, al-Razi recognized the urgent need for a coherent framework that would organize this vast intellectual landscape. His classification was not merely an administrative exercise; it was a profound reflection on the nature of knowledge itself.

IN *AL-MATALIB AL-'ALIYA*, al-Razi delineates various branches of learning, distinguishing between those that are empirical in nature and those that are of a more abstract, philosophical character. He identifies the hierarchy of sciences, proposing that some disciplines provide the foundational principles upon which others build. At the base of this hierarchy lie the natural sciences, derived largely from sensory experience, which must be supplemented by the more rigorous and reflective disciplines of logic and metaphysics.

. . .

AL-RAZI'S CLASSIFICATION GOES FURTHER, proposing that certain sciences—such as theology and metaphysics—occupy a special position. These disciplines address questions that are not readily answered by empirical observation alone, dealing instead with the ultimate causes and the transcendent aspects of reality. This hierarchy, with its implicit recognition of different modes of inquiry, underscores the idea that human knowledge is multifaceted and that no single method can claim exclusive authority over the truth.

MOREOVER, the systemization of knowledge in *Al-Matalib al-'Aliya* reflects al-Razi's broader epistemological vision: that the pursuit of knowledge is both a practical and a spiritual endeavor. By categorizing the sciences, he provides a roadmap for scholars, guiding them from the concrete observations of the world to the abstract principles that govern it. This classification not only facilitates intellectual inquiry but also harmonizes the diverse sources of knowledge, affirming that each contributes to the collective understanding of reality.

CONCLUSION

THE EXPLORATION of the sources of human knowledge, as illuminated by al-Razi, reveals a dynamic interplay between sensory experience, reason, revelation, and systematic classification. Sense perception, with all its immediacy and limitations, provides the raw material from which knowledge begins. Reason refines this material, elevating it to the level of universal principles through rigorous analysis and dialectical inquiry. Yet, it is through the light of revelation that the mind accesses truths that lie beyond empirical reach, imbuing human understanding with a sacred dimension.

Al-Razi's systematic classification of the sciences, as articulated in *Al-Matalib al-'Aliya*, brings coherence to this multifaceted epistemological framework. It is a reminder that knowledge is not a singular pursuit but a diverse field in which different methods, each with its own strengths and limitations, must be integrated to form a comprehensive vision of reality.

In embracing these varied sources, al-Razi not only charts a course for intellectual inquiry but also sets an enduring standard for the balance between the empirical and the transcendental—a balance that continues to inspire the quest for wisdom across cultures and epochs.

4
THE NATURE OF TRUTH AND CERTAINTY

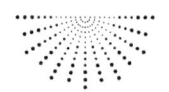

In this chapter, we embark on a rigorous inquiry into one of the most enduring questions of philosophy: What is truth, and how can we attain certainty in our knowledge? Drawing upon al-Razi's expansive intellectual legacy, this discussion unpacks varied definitions of truth, examines the spectrum of certainty in human understanding, and critically engages with skepticism—both its appeal and its shortcomings. Al-Razi's methodical approach to these questions not only shaped medieval thought but continues to resonate with modern debates in epistemology.

Definitions of Truth

Truth, as al-Razi envisioned it, is neither a static abstraction nor a mere label for the observable phenomena of the world. Instead, it is an evolving, multifaceted concept that integrates empirical reality with metaphysical depth. Al-Razi argued that truth is not simply what appears to be true at first glance but what withstands the scrutiny of reason and revelation alike.

At its most basic level, truth can be seen as the correspondence between our beliefs or statements and the actual state of affairs. However, al-Razi challenged this simplistic correspondence theory by suggesting that the human encounter with truth is always mediated by our cognitive faculties. Our senses provide us with raw data, and our reason processes this data, filtering it through preconceived notions, cultural contexts, and logical structures. Thus, for al-Razi, the search for truth is an active process—one that demands careful examination and persistent inquiry.

Moreover, al-Razi distinguished between relative truths, which pertain to everyday experiences, and absolute truths that reside in the realm of the metaphysical. While the former are contingent upon sensory perceptions and personal interpretations, the latter are accessible only through a synthesis of reason and divine revelation. This dual-layered conception of truth invites a deeper exploration: it encourages the thinker to question not only what is immediately evident but also to pursue a more profound understanding that transcends ordinary perception.

In articulating these definitions, al-Razi did not claim to provide definitive answers but rather to illuminate the pathways that lead closer to a comprehensive grasp of reality. His approach emphasizes that truth is a pursuit rather than a destination—one that must be continually refined as new insights emerge.

DEGREES OF CERTAINTY

WHILE THE QUEST for truth is central to intellectual inquiry, al-Razi recognized that not all truths are known with equal assurance. He proposed a nuanced theory of certainty, one that acknowledges the gradations in the reliability of our knowledge. This perspective challenges the binary view of truth as either absolutely certain or entirely uncertain, suggesting instead a spectrum of confidence.

AT ONE END of the spectrum lie the insights gained from direct sensory experience and well-tested empirical observations. These are the kinds of truths that, while not infallible, are supported by consistent evidence and are generally accepted by the community of scholars. However, even these truths are subject to refinement. As new information comes to light or as analytical methods improve, what was once held as a near-certain fact may be reinterpreted or even overturned.

MOVING FURTHER ALONG THE SPECTRUM, al-Razi highlights the role of rational deductions and logical proofs. These forms of knowledge, derived from systematic reasoning, often possess a higher degree of certainty than empirical observations alone, because they are less susceptible to the vagaries of perception. Yet, even logical deductions are not immune to critique. The possibility of hidden assumptions, unexamined premises, or logical fallacies means that each conclusion must be open to revision in light of new arguments or counterexamples.

AT THE HIGHEST level of certainty, according to al-Razi, reside the truths that are revealed through divine insight. These revelations, often conveyed through sacred texts and prophetic teachings, provide a bedrock of knowledge that supports and transcends human reason. However, even here, al-Razi warns against complacency; the interpretation of revelation must be continually subjected to critical scrutiny, ensuring that it is harmonized with the rational and empirical dimensions of human experience.

THIS GRADATIONAL MODEL of certainty underscores a key element of al-Razi's philosophy: the understanding that human knowledge is provisional and ever-evolving. By recognizing degrees of certainty, scholars are encouraged to maintain a balance between confidence and humility—a balance that allows for both the celebration of what is known and the anticipation of further discovery.

SKEPTICISM and Its Refutation

NO DISCOURSE on truth and certainty would be complete without confronting skepticism—the view that questions the possibility of achieving any true or certain knowledge. Skepticism, in its various forms, has long posed a formidable challenge to those who claim to know the truth. Al-Razi was acutely aware of this challenge and devoted considerable effort to both understanding and refuting skeptical arguments.

SKEPTICS ARGUE that our senses are fallible, our reasoning can be flawed, and that even divine revelation may be misinterpreted. This cascade of doubts leads to a radical uncertainty, suggesting that absolute certainty might be an unattainable ideal. For some, such skepticism may even verge on nihilism, implying that if certainty is impossible, then so too is the pursuit of knowledge.

IN RESPONSE, al-Razi offered a robust critique of skepticism. He contended that while skepticism rightly exposes the limitations inherent in human cognition, it fails to account for the cumulative and corrective nature of the human quest for understanding. In other words, the very process of inquiry—characterized by testing, questioning, and refining ideas—serves as a bulwark against the paralysis of doubt. Rather than viewing skepticism as a terminal condition, al-Razi saw it as a temporary stage in the progressive journey towards more secure knowledge.

ONE OF THE key elements in his refutation is the concept of "incremental certainty." By embracing a model where certainty is acquired in degrees, al-Razi demonstrates that even if absolute certainty remains elusive, one can still achieve a high level of confidence in many areas of inquiry. This incremental approach allows for a pragmatic acceptance of knowledge that is sufficiently reliable for both practical purposes and further intellectual development.

MOREOVER, al-Razi argued that the very act of engaging with skepticism fortifies the integrity of knowledge. When ideas are subjected to rigorous challenge and debate, only those that can withstand such scrutiny emerge as robust. This dialectical process not only refines individual beliefs but also contributes to a broader, more resilient body of knowledge. By transforming skepticism into a tool for improvement rather than a weapon of perpetual doubt, al-Razi provided a powerful framework for intellectual progress.

Finally, al-Razi's integration of divine revelation into his epistemology offers another avenue for refuting skepticism. While human reason may falter, the truths illuminated by revelation provide an external point of reference—a divine standard against which human fallibility can be measured and corrected. In this way, the interplay of reason, empirical observation, and revelation forms a comprehensive response to the challenges posed by skepticism.

Conclusion

Chapter 4 has explored the intricate nature of truth and the pursuit of certainty as envisaged by al-Razi. By examining the layered definitions of truth, the spectrum of certainty, and the formidable challenge of skepticism, we gain insight into a philosophical tradition that is both rigorous and adaptable. Al-Razi's thought invites us to see knowledge as a dynamic process—one that is continuously refined through experience, logical analysis, and the illumination of divine insight.

In embracing this multifaceted approach, al-Razi not only defends the possibility of achieving reliable knowledge but also celebrates the enduring journey of inquiry. The recognition that truth is approached incrementally, and that skepticism, when properly engaged, serves as a catalyst for deeper understanding, remains a powerful legacy for all who seek to reconcile the complexities of human thought with the profound mysteries of existence.

5
LOGIC AND DIALECTIC

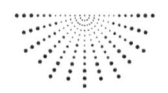

IN THE QUEST FOR TRUTH, LOGIC EMERGES NOT MERELY AS AN instrument but as the very framework through which the intricacies of existence are parsed and understood. This chapter delves into the essential role that logic and dialectic play in intellectual inquiry, examining how these tools enable scholars to dissect, analyze, and ultimately reconcile the manifold aspects of knowledge. We begin by exploring the overarching significance of logic, proceed to survey al-Razi's innovative contributions to this discipline, and finally, consider the refined art of disputation—a method through which conflicting ideas are harmonized in pursuit of deeper understanding.

THE IMPORTANCE of Logic in Intellectual Inquiry

LOGIC STANDS as the bedrock of all rigorous intellectual endeavor. It is the disciplined method by which ideas are organized, evaluated, and refined. At its core, logic provides the structure necessary to separate the valid from the spurious, the essential from the accidental. In every field—from mathematics and the natural sciences to theology and philosophy—the application of logical principles ensures that inquiry is not mired in ambiguity or error.

IN THE REALM of intellectual inquiry, logic serves a dual purpose. Firstly, it functions as a clarifying tool, stripping away the layers of opinion and subjective bias to reveal the underlying structure of thought. Secondly, it operates as a system of accountability; every argument, no matter how brilliant, must be subjected to the scrutiny of logical consistency. In doing so, logic not only safeguards the integrity of knowledge but also fosters a culture of critical engagement, where ideas are continually tested against the standards of coherence and rationality.

THROUGHOUT HISTORY, the development of logical methods has paralleled the evolution of human thought. The methodical examination of cause and effect, the systematic categorization of propositions, and the precise formulation of arguments have all contributed to a legacy in which logic is both a tool and a goal. In this context, logic is not seen as an abstract or sterile discipline but as a vibrant and dynamic process that fuels the advancement of understanding. By enforcing a rigorous standard of thought, logic empowers scholars to navigate the complex interplay between empirical data, theoretical frameworks, and the timeless questions of existence.

AL-RAZI'S CONTRIBUTIONS to Logic

. . .

AL-RAZI'S WORK in the field of logic is emblematic of his broader commitment to the harmonization of faith and reason. At a time when many of his contemporaries accepted traditional modes of thought uncritically, al-Razi sought to challenge and refine these paradigms by integrating the logical traditions inherited from Greek philosophy with innovative approaches rooted in his own empirical and theological insights.

ONE OF AL-RAZI'S key contributions was his insistence that logical inquiry must be adaptive and context-sensitive. While he respected the classical methods of syllogistic reasoning and deductive analysis, he was equally aware of their limitations when confronted with the multifaceted nature of reality. As such, he advocated for a more flexible approach—one that could accommodate both the precision of formal logic and the more fluid, dialectical methods necessary for grappling with metaphysical questions.

AL-RAZI'S TREATISES on logic demonstrate his skill in dissecting complex arguments and reconstructing them in a way that highlights their inherent contradictions and possibilities. He was particularly adept at identifying hidden assumptions and fallacious reasoning, thereby clearing the path for more robust and resilient theories. His work often involved a meticulous reexamination of accepted premises, urging scholars not to take for granted that well-established ideas were immune to doubt or reinterpretation.

FURTHERMORE, al-Razi's contributions extended to the realm of symbolic representation and classification. In his efforts to systematize various branches of knowledge, he laid the groundwork for a more unified approach to intellectual inquiry—one where logic served as the common language bridging disparate disciplines. His integrative vision underscored the belief that no single domain of thought could claim exclusivity over truth; rather, all fields must be held to the same standards of rational examination.

Through his pioneering work in logic, al-Razi not only enriched the intellectual landscape of his time but also provided enduring methodologies that continue to influence modern debates in epistemology, philosophy, and science. His legacy in logic is a testament to the power of reason to illuminate the deepest mysteries of existence, guiding the seeker through the labyrinth of ideas with clarity and precision.

The Art of Disputation

Beyond the formal structures of logic lies the art of disputation—a method of intellectual engagement that transforms debate into a constructive, even transformative, process. For al-Razi, disputation was far more than a mere clash of opinions; it was an essential mechanism by which truth could be distilled from the interplay of conflicting perspectives.

The art of disputation involves a delicate balance: it requires both assertiveness in defending one's position and openness to the insights that emerge from opposing viewpoints. In al-Razi's view, every argument, when subjected to rigorous dialectical exchange, has the potential to reveal new layers of meaning. This process of dialectic—where thesis and antithesis engage in a dynamic interplay—serves to refine ideas rather than simply discredit them. Through well-structured debate, participants are invited to identify common ground, resolve apparent contradictions, and ultimately arrive at a synthesis that is more nuanced than the original positions.

AL-RAZI'S APPROACH to disputation is marked by a commitment to clarity and precision. He insisted that every claim should be supported by clear evidence and sound reasoning, and that no idea should be immune to scrutiny. This method not only fortified the arguments he advanced but also elevated the overall quality of intellectual discourse. Disputation, under his guidance, was a collaborative pursuit of truth, a shared endeavor where adversaries in argument could become co-travelers in the journey towards greater understanding.

MOREOVER, al-Razi was keenly aware of the pedagogical value of disputation. By engaging in structured debates, scholars are not only forced to articulate their views with precision but are also given the opportunity to learn from the insights of others. In this respect, disputation becomes a form of intellectual alchemy, transforming the raw material of disagreement into the refined gold of knowledge. It encourages humility, fosters critical thinking, and cultivates an environment in which ideas are continuously tested and improved.

THE ART of disputation also serves a broader societal function. In a world where dogmatism and unchallenged authority can stifle innovation and suppress dissent, the practice of reasoned debate offers a powerful antidote. It champions a culture in which ideas must earn their place through merit and logical coherence, rather than relying on tradition or power. This democratic spirit of inquiry, so ardently promoted by al-Razi, remains a cornerstone of intellectual freedom and progress.

Conclusion

The exploration of logic and dialectic in this chapter reveals a profound commitment to the rigorous pursuit of truth—a commitment that lies at the heart of al-Razi's intellectual legacy. By emphasizing the indispensable role of logic in organizing and scrutinizing ideas, al-Razi set a high standard for intellectual inquiry, one that continues to resonate across disciplines. His innovative contributions to the field of logic not only refined the methods of argumentation but also laid the groundwork for a more integrated and holistic approach to knowledge.

Equally significant is his articulation of the art of disputation—a method that transforms conflict into collaboration, where the meeting of opposing views becomes a catalyst for deeper understanding. Through this process, the seemingly disparate strands of human thought are woven into a coherent tapestry, each debate a step towards the illumination of truth.

In embracing both the formal rigor of logic and the dynamic interplay of dialectic, al-Razi leaves us with a legacy that is as much about the method of inquiry as it is about its ultimate aims. His work invites us to continue questioning, to engage critically with every idea, and to recognize that the pursuit of truth is an ever-evolving journey—one in which logic and disputation serve as both compass and map in the unending exploration of the human intellect.

6
THE EXISTENCE OF GOD

This chapter embarks on one of the most profound inquiries in the history of human thought—the question of God's existence. Far from a mere abstract debate, the issue of divine existence lies at the heart of metaphysical, ethical, and cosmological discourse. Drawing upon the intellectual rigor of al-Razi, we shall explore a diverse array of arguments that affirm the existence of God, while also engaging critically with contemporary challenges such as atheism and materialism. Through reasoned analysis, empirical observation, and the integration of revealed wisdom, al-Razi's thought provides a rich tapestry of insights that seek to bridge the human experience with the transcendent.

Arguments for God's Existence

The Cosmological Perspective

One of the foundational arguments for God's existence, as elaborated by al-Razi, is rooted in the observation of the cosmos itself. The universe, with its intricate order, dynamic processes, and ceaseless evolution, stands as a testament to the existence of a prime mover—a necessary cause that transcends the temporal and contingent. Al-Razi posited that every effect, no matter how grand or minute, must have a cause. This causal chain, when traced back far enough, inevitably points to a first cause—one that is uncaused, eternal, and self-sufficient. This prime mover, he argued, must be God.

In his reflections on the natural world, al-Razi emphasized that the orderly arrangement of celestial bodies, the precision of natural laws, and the harmonious interdependence of cosmic elements are not products of random chance but are indicative of an intelligent design. This cosmological argument extends beyond the observable to the metaphysical, suggesting that the very possibility of a universe that exists in a state of coherence implies the guiding hand of a divine creator.

The Teleological Argument

Complementing the cosmological viewpoint is the teleological or design argument, which asserts that the purpose and functionality inherent in the natural world point to a deliberate design. Al-Razi observed that the universe exhibits a remarkable degree of fine-tuning, where the constants of nature and the structures of matter seem perfectly calibrated to support complex forms of life. In this light, the existence of intricate systems—from the microscopic to the cosmic—cannot be adequately explained by mere chance. Instead, they call for the presence of an intelligent agent whose wisdom and foresight are manifest in the design of creation.

Al-Razi's teleological reflections extend to the human realm, where the very capacities for reason, creativity, and moral judgment are seen as reflections of a higher, divine order. The beauty and symmetry of the natural world, the cyclic patterns of life and death, and the progression of human civilization are all viewed as part of a grand, purposeful plan. This perspective underscores the idea that the universe is not a haphazard collection of matter but a meticulously orchestrated system that mirrors the attributes of its Creator.

The Moral Argument

Another compelling line of reasoning in support of God's existence is found in the moral argument. Al-Razi contended that the existence of objective moral values and duties points toward a transcendent source. In a world where right and wrong could be subjectively determined, the presence of universal ethical principles—the shared understanding of justice, compassion, and human dignity—suggests an origin beyond the confines of individual or cultural preferences.

For al-Razi, morality is not a social construct but an enduring truth, imbued with the authority of divine revelation. The moral order, he argued, is a reflection of God's nature—a perfect standard against which all human actions can be measured. This argument posits that without a divine foundation, moral values would be arbitrary and subject to the whims of changing social conditions. Instead, the existence of a stable moral framework is best explained by the presence of an omnipotent, omniscient God who instills in humanity an innate sense of justice and righteousness.

The Argument from Contingency

A further dimension in al-Razi's argument for God's existence lies in the observation of contingency in the universe. Everything that exists within the realm of the contingent—those entities that come into being and pass away—requires an explanation for why it exists rather than not. Al-Razi maintained that the sheer fact of contingent existence points toward a necessary being whose existence is not dependent on anything else. This necessary being, by contrast to the contingent, must exist by its very nature, serving as the ultimate source of all that is.

This line of reasoning is deeply intertwined with the metaphysical investigations into the nature of existence. It invites us to consider that if every contingent thing requires a cause, then the chain of causation must ultimately culminate in a being that is self-existent and necessary. For al-Razi, this being is none other than God—a being whose existence is not subject to the limitations and uncertainties that characterize all other entities.

Critique of Atheism and Materialism

. . .

Challenging Reductionism

AT THE HEART of atheism and materialism lies the assertion that all phenomena can be reduced to physical processes and empirical observations. Proponents of this view often claim that the complexities of life, consciousness, and the cosmos can be entirely explained by the interactions of matter and energy, with no need to invoke a supernatural cause. Al-Razi, however, challenges this reductionist perspective by arguing that material explanations alone are insufficient to capture the full spectrum of human experience and the nature of reality.

AL-RAZI'S CRITIQUE begins with the observation that while materialism can describe how things function, it fails to explain why they exist in the first place. The laws of nature, though precise and consistent, do not account for the origin of these very laws or the initial conditions that made the emergence of a structured universe possible. Moreover, the reductionist approach tends to disregard the qualitative dimensions of human life—such as consciousness, morality, and the experience of beauty—which point toward a reality that transcends the material.

The Limits of Empirical Inquiry

EMPIRICAL METHODS HAVE UNDOUBTEDLY YIELDED profound insights into the workings of the natural world. However, al-Razi cautioned against the assumption that empirical inquiry is the sole path to knowledge. While the senses and scientific instruments provide us with data about the physical universe, they are inherently limited in their capacity to capture metaphysical truths. The existence of God, as argued by al-Razi, is a conclusion that rests on the interplay of empirical observation, logical deduction, and revelatory insight—a synthesis that materialism, with its strict empirical focus, cannot accommodate.

AL-RAZI ARGUED that the reliance on empirical evidence alone leads to a truncated view of reality. The nuances of existence—such as the unity of the cosmos, the nature of moral values, and the emergence of self-awareness—demand a broader epistemological approach. By acknowledging the limitations of sensory perception and the finite scope of scientific inquiry, al-Razi opens the door to a more expansive understanding of truth, one that encompasses the transcendent dimensions of being.

ETHICAL AND EXISTENTIAL **Implications**

THE REJECTION of God's existence, as advanced by atheism and materialism, carries significant ethical and existential implications. Without a divine foundation, the source of objective moral values becomes tenuous, leaving society to grapple with a relativistic ethics that fluctuates with cultural and temporal shifts. Al-Razi maintained that the absence of a transcendent moral standard undermines the very basis of justice, compassion, and human dignity.

FURTHERMORE, the materialistic worldview can lead to a sense of existential nihilism—a belief that life is ultimately devoid of meaning or purpose. Al-Razi countered that the recognition of a divine purpose not only imbues human life with significance but also provides a framework within which suffering, joy, and the myriad experiences of life can be understood in relation to a higher order. In this light, the existence of God is not only a metaphysical claim but also an ethical imperative that sustains the human spirit in the face of adversity.

Integrative Reflections

In his critique of atheism and materialism, al-Razi does not simply dismiss these views as erroneous; rather, he engages them in a dialectical process that seeks to integrate the valid insights of empirical science with the deeper questions of existence. He acknowledges the remarkable achievements of material inquiry while simultaneously advocating for an understanding that embraces both the seen and the unseen, the measurable and the ineffable.

Al-Razi's integrative approach insists that the pursuit of truth is not an either/or proposition. Instead, it is a journey that navigates the rich interplay between reason, revelation, and empirical observation. The limitations of a purely materialistic perspective, he argued, highlight the necessity of a more holistic worldview—one that recognizes the existence of a transcendent reality and the profound implications of that reality for both knowledge and ethics.

Conclusion

. . .

In this chapter, we have traversed the profound terrain of the question of God's existence as illuminated by al-Razi's thought. From the cosmological and teleological arguments that evoke the grandeur of the cosmos to the moral and contingent dimensions that underscore the necessity of a divine presence, the evidence for God emerges as a compelling tapestry woven from multiple strands of inquiry.

Al-Razi's rigorous critique of atheism and materialism further reinforces this vision by exposing the limitations of a worldview that confines itself solely to the material realm. His reflections invite us to appreciate that the pursuit of truth is an intricate process—one that harmonizes empirical observations with metaphysical insights, and that acknowledges both the power and the limitations of human reason.

Ultimately, the exploration of divine existence in al-Razi's philosophy is a call to transcend narrow perspectives and embrace a more comprehensive understanding of reality. It is a journey that challenges us to look beyond the visible, to question the assumptions of our time, and to seek a truth that is as expansive and enduring as the cosmos itself.

7
THE DIVINE ATTRIBUTES

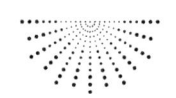

IN THIS CHAPTER, WE DELVE INTO ONE OF THE MOST PROFOUND dimensions of theological inquiry: the nature and attributes of the Divine. Al-Razi's approach to the divine is marked by a nuanced understanding that transcends simplistic dichotomies. He meticulously distinguishes between the positive attributes that express God's active presence in the cosmos and the negative attributes which affirm the transcendence and ineffability of the Divine essence. In doing so, al-Razi not only redefines the contours of traditional theology but also lays the groundwork for a more sophisticated dialogue on the nature of God—one that avoids the pitfalls of anthropomorphism while celebrating the mystery of divine perfection.

POSITIVE ATTRIBUTES: Manifestations of Divine Excellence

AL-RAZI POSITS that the positive attributes of God—such as Knowledge, Power, and Will—are not mere abstract qualities but dynamic manifestations that infuse creation with order and purpose.

Knowledge

For al-Razi, divine Knowledge is absolute and all-encompassing. It is not confined by the limitations of human understanding but rather is the very foundation upon which the universe is built. This omniscience is evident in the intricate design of the cosmos, where every element, from the smallest particle to the grandest celestial body, operates in harmony with universal laws. Divine Knowledge, in his view, illuminates the path of creation, ensuring that every phenomenon has its rightful place and purpose. It serves as the ultimate source of wisdom, guiding the unfolding of events in a manner that is both orderly and profoundly mysterious.

Power

Divine Power, another cardinal attribute, is understood as the capacity to bring forth existence and sustain it against the chaos of non-being. Al-Razi sees this power as manifest in the natural laws that govern the universe—laws that are both consistent and remarkably precise. This power is not coercive in the human sense; instead, it operates with a subtle, underlying force that permeates all aspects of reality. It is the creative energy that enables transformation and renewal, the force that underwrites both the stability and the dynamism of the cosmos. In al-Razi's framework, divine Power assures that the universe is not a static collection of atoms, but a living, evolving tapestry in which every moment is charged with potential and purpose.

WILL

THE DIVINE WILL is the organizing principle behind the intentionality of creation. It is the faculty through which God exercises purpose and direction in the cosmos. Unlike human will, which is often fraught with ambiguity and conflict, the Divine Will is singular and harmonious. It ensures that all events, however disparate they may seem, are interwoven into a coherent narrative that reflects the ultimate good. For al-Razi, the Divine Will is both the initiator and the sustainer of all that exists; it is the subtle force that imparts meaning to the seemingly random occurrences of nature, transforming them into expressions of a grand, purposeful design.

NEGATIVE ATTRIBUTES and the Transcendence of God (Asas al-Taqdis)

WHILE THE POSITIVE attributes provide a window into the operational aspects of the Divine, al-Razi's theology is equally concerned with the negative attributes—those characteristics that underscore God's transcendence and ultimate ineffability. This concept, often encapsulated in the notion of *Asas al-Taqdis* (the foundation of sanctification), is central to understanding how the Divine is both immanent in creation and wholly distinct from it.

. . .

Beyond Human Limitations

Al-Razi was keenly aware of the dangers inherent in attributing human qualities to the Divine. To avoid reducing God to a mere superlative human figure, he employed the method of negation—a process by which one delineates what God is not, rather than attempting to capture the fullness of divine essence in positive terms. In doing so, al-Razi affirmed that while God may be described in terms of power, knowledge, and will, these descriptors should not be understood in any human sense. Instead, they point to a reality that is infinitely greater than any creaturely approximation.

The Ineffability of the Divine Essence

Central to *Asas al-Taqdis* is the belief that the divine essence remains utterly inaccessible to human perception and comprehension. The negative attributes thus serve as a safeguard against the overreach of human language and conceptualization. They remind us that any attempt to define God in finite terms is inherently limited. God's transcendence means that while we may glimpse aspects of the Divine through creation and revelation, the ultimate nature of God escapes all definitive description. This approach preserves the sanctity and mystery of the Divine, ensuring that worship remains an encounter with the ineffable, rather than a reduction to simplistic categories.

A Framework for Theological Humility

. . .

By emphasizing what God is not, al-Razi cultivates a sense of theological humility. Recognizing that the Divine transcends all human attributes instills a cautious reverence in the believer. It is a call to approach the mysteries of faith with an openness to the unknown and a willingness to embrace paradox. In this framework, the process of understanding God becomes less about accumulating a list of qualities and more about engaging in an ongoing dialogue with the mystery of existence—a dialogue that acknowledges the limits of human knowledge and celebrates the boundless nature of the Divine.

The Problem of Anthropomorphism

One of the perennial challenges in theological discourse is the risk of anthropomorphism: the tendency to ascribe human characteristics to the Divine. Al-Razi was particularly sensitive to this issue and devoted significant attention to delineating the boundaries between metaphor and literal description.

The Lure of Familiarity

Anthropomorphic language offers a comforting familiarity; it allows humans to relate to the Divine in terms they can understand. However, this familiarity is a double-edged sword. While it facilitates an emotional and intellectual connection, it also risks distorting the true nature of God. Al-Razi argued that to reduce God to human terms is to confine the infinite to the finite—to capture the boundless essence of the Divine within the narrow limits of human experience. This reduction not only misrepresents God but also undermines the transformative potential of encountering a truly transcendent reality.

Critical Examination of Metaphorical Language

In response to the allure of anthropomorphism, al-Razi adopted a critical stance towards language itself. He maintained that metaphors, while useful as pedagogical tools, must be employed with caution. They are, after all, imperfect instruments for conveying the ineffable. The risk lies in allowing metaphor to become literal, thereby diminishing the profound mystery that characterizes the Divine. For al-Razi, it was essential to maintain a clear distinction between the symbolic and the literal—to use human language as a guide rather than a definitive statement of divine reality.

Preserving the Integrity of Divine Transcendence

To counteract the tendency towards anthropomorphism, al-Razi proposed a method of theological interpretation that emphasizes both the positive and negative attributes of God in a balanced manner. This method ensures that while the Divine is approachable and relatable through certain attributes, the core essence of God remains utterly transcendent. In doing so, he preserves the integrity of divine transcendence, affirming that God is not merely an exalted version of humanity but a reality that exceeds all human understanding. This approach not only safeguards the majesty of the Divine but also enriches the believer's spiritual experience by inviting an encounter with a reality that is both immanent and wholly other.

Conclusion

Chapter 7 has taken us on an in-depth exploration of the divine attributes as conceived by al-Razi—a journey that traverses the fertile ground between the known and the ineffable. The positive attributes of Knowledge, Power, and Will reveal a God who is actively engaged in the orchestration of the cosmos, imbuing creation with order, purpose, and vitality. Yet, these attributes are complemented by the negative attributes encapsulated in the notion of *Asas al-Taqdis*, which remind us of the profound transcendence and sanctity of the Divine essence.

By carefully distinguishing between what can be affirmed about God and what must remain a mystery, al-Razi provides a model for understanding that is both rich in intellectual rigor and deeply respectful of the limits of human comprehension. His critique of anthropomorphism serves as a timeless reminder that while language is an invaluable tool for expressing spiritual truths, it must always be wielded with an awareness of its inherent limitations.

In embracing both the revealed and the ineffable, al-Razi's theology invites us to engage in a dialogue with the Divine that is as much about the mystery of what lies beyond as it is about the illumination of what is known. It is an invitation to a faith that is dynamic, humble, and ever open to the wondrous complexity of existence—a faith that continues to inspire and challenge seekers of truth across the ages.

8
DIVINE ACTION AND PROVIDENCE

IN THIS CHAPTER, WE DELVE INTO THE INTRICATE DYNAMICS OF divine action—a realm where the transcendent meets the temporal, and where the mysterious interplay of destiny and free will is brought into sharp relief. Al-Razi's exploration of divine action and providence offers a multifaceted vision of God's relationship with the world, the unfolding of a divine decree that governs cosmic order, and the simultaneous affirmation of human free will and moral responsibility. In grappling with these questions, al-Razi invites us to consider how a transcendent, omniscient Creator can be intimately involved in the everyday affairs of the universe without compromising the autonomy and dignity of human beings.

GOD'S RELATIONSHIP with the World

THE IMMANENCE of the Divine

. . .

AL-RAZI'S THOUGHT asserts that God is not an aloof or detached entity, distant from the affairs of creation, but is instead intimately involved with the world. This immanence is evident in the natural order, where every event, every phenomenon, and every act of creation bears the mark of a divine presence. In al-Razi's view, the universe is a reflection of divine wisdom, its order and beauty testifying to a higher purpose. Every aspect of nature—from the rhythm of the celestial bodies to the intricacies of biological life—echoes the creative act of God, suggesting that nothing occurs by chance.

The Sustaining Power of Providence

FOR AL-RAZI, the world is sustained by a continuous, life-affirming force—a divine providence that nurtures, guides, and, when necessary, intervenes in the course of natural events. This sustaining power does not override natural laws; rather, it operates through them, ensuring that creation unfolds according to a harmonious plan. In this schema, divine action is both the originator of cosmic order and the guarantor of its persistence. Every unfolding event in the cosmos, whether miraculous or mundane, is seen as part of a grand tapestry, woven by a Creator whose hand is evident in every detail.

The Interplay Between Transcendence and Immanence

AL-RAZI IS careful to maintain a delicate balance between the transcendence of God and His immanence in the world. While God is utterly beyond the confines of space and time,

He remains accessible to the world through the signs of creation and the rhythm of providence. This duality—being both wholly other and intimately present—defines the nature of divine action. It suggests that the divine is not confined to abstract theological musings but is actively engaged in the ongoing drama of existence. Every natural law, every contingent event, and every moment of human experience is imbued with a trace of the divine, even as God's essence remains transcendent and ineffable.

The Nature of Divine Decree and Predestination

The Concept of Divine Decree

Central to al-Razi's understanding of divine action is the notion of the divine decree—a preordained plan that governs the order of the universe. This decree is not a rigid script that leaves no room for deviation; rather, it is a dynamic framework within which the myriad events of the world occur. God's decree is the ultimate expression of divine wisdom, reflecting an order that is both rational and purposeful. It encompasses all things, from the grand movements of celestial bodies to the minute details of everyday life, ensuring that every occurrence, whether joyous or tragic, has its rightful place in the cosmic scheme.

Predestination: Determinism Revisited

The concept of predestination has long provoked debate among scholars and theologians. In al-Razi's framework, predestination is understood as the logical consequence of a universe that operates under a coherent, divinely instituted order. Every event is, in principle, part of a pre-established plan—a tapestry woven by the Creator. Yet, al-Razi's treatment of predestination is nuanced. He recognizes that while God's decree sets the parameters within which creation unfolds, it does not annihilate the capacity for change, growth, or human deliberation. The divine plan is flexible enough to incorporate the unfolding of events in a manner that respects both cosmic order and individual agency.

Reconciling Apparent Paradoxes

One of the enduring challenges in discussions of divine decree is reconciling the apparent tension between determinism and human freedom. Critics of predestination argue that if all events are foreordained, then human actions become mere illusions of choice, stripping individuals of moral responsibility. Al-Razi, however, offers a sophisticated perspective that resolves this tension by distinguishing between the general framework of divine decree and the particularities of human action. While the broader strokes of destiny are set in motion by God's will, the finer details—especially those concerning moral choices—are left to the autonomous deliberation of human beings. In this way, al-Razi upholds the notion that divine predestination does not negate the authenticity of human experience or the accountability of human actions.

Human Free Will and Responsibility

. . .

The Autonomy of the Human Spirit

Al-Razi champions the idea that human beings possess an inherent capacity for free will—a faculty that allows them to choose, deliberate, and act according to their own rational judgments. This capacity is not an accidental by-product of creation but a deliberate gift bestowed upon humanity. The freedom to choose is what elevates human existence, providing the means for moral growth, self-improvement, and the pursuit of virtue. In al-Razi's thought, free will is integral to the human condition, affirming that each individual has the power to shape their destiny within the contours of divine providence.

Moral Responsibility and Accountability

With the gift of free will comes the responsibility for one's actions. Al-Razi is adamant that human freedom is inextricably linked to moral accountability. Every choice made by an individual carries with it the weight of responsibility—ethical and spiritual. This responsibility is not arbitrary; it is rooted in the belief that human actions have real consequences, both in this life and beyond. In a universe governed by divine decree, the exercise of free will is the arena in which moral values are both tested and actualized. Human beings, through their choices, have the opportunity to participate in the ongoing work of creation, aligning themselves with the divine will or deviating from the path of righteousness.

The Synergy of Divine Providence and Human Agency

. . .

Perhaps the most compelling aspect of al-Razi's vision is the way in which he harmonizes divine providence with human agency. He contends that divine action and human freedom are not mutually exclusive but operate in a synergistic relationship. God, in His infinite wisdom, has established a framework that both guides and supports human endeavor. Within this framework, individuals are endowed with the capacity to make choices that reflect their inner moral and intellectual convictions. While the overarching structure of existence is maintained by divine decree, the details of individual lives are animated by the creative force of free will. This synergy ensures that while destiny provides the canvas, it is human choice that paints the intricate details of life's portrait.

Embracing the Mystery

Despite the intellectual rigor with which al-Razi examines these issues, he is ever mindful of the limits of human understanding. The precise mechanisms by which divine decree and free will interact remain, to some extent, a mystery—a mystery that invites continual reflection, debate, and wonder. Al-Razi does not claim to have resolved every tension inherent in this interplay; rather, he encourages an approach that balances confidence in divine wisdom with humility in the face of the unknown. This balanced perspective is a hallmark of his thought, inviting scholars and seekers alike to engage in a lifelong journey of inquiry where every question opens the door to deeper understanding.

. . .

Conclusion

CHAPTER 8 HAS EXPLORED the multifaceted dimensions of divine action and providence as envisioned by al-Razi. By examining God's intimate relationship with the world, the nature of divine decree and predestination, and the pivotal role of human free will and responsibility, we gain insight into a worldview that is both deterministic and liberating. Al-Razi's approach demonstrates that the divine is neither a distant puppeteer nor an indifferent observer, but an active, sustaining force that works in concert with human agency.

THIS SYNTHESIS of divine governance and human freedom challenges us to rethink our understanding of fate and responsibility. It asserts that while the cosmos is ordered by an overarching divine plan, the details of our lives are ours to shape through our choices and actions. In this interplay, we find a profound affirmation of human dignity, moral accountability, and the potential for growth—a testament to the enduring legacy of al-Razi's thought, which continues to inspire seekers of truth and wisdom across the ages.

9
THE STRUCTURE OF THE UNIVERSE

IN THIS CHAPTER, WE DELVE INTO ONE OF THE MOST compelling arenas of intellectual inquiry—cosmology. Central to al-Razi's thought is his deep engagement with the structure of the universe, a subject that demanded a critical reassessment of the prevailing astronomical models. With rigorous critique and inventive theorization, al-Razi challenged the long-held Ptolemaic framework and put forth alternative cosmological models in his treatise *Mabahith al-Mashriqiyya*. His reflections on the cosmos not only redefined the parameters of scientific and philosophical inquiry in his time but also anticipated later developments in astronomical thought.

CRITIQUE OF PTOLEMAIC Astronomy

QUESTIONING ESTABLISHED Paradigms

. . .

The Ptolemaic system, which had dominated astronomical thought for centuries, was built on a geocentric model in which the Earth was considered the immovable center of the universe. According to this framework, the planets, stars, and celestial spheres revolved around the Earth in complex orbits that sought to reconcile observable motions with the ideal of circular perfection. Yet, al-Razi was not content with accepting this model at face value. He scrutinized its underlying assumptions with a critical eye, questioning whether the apparent orderliness of the cosmos could truly be accounted for by a system that placed the Earth at its core.

Al-Razi argued that the Ptolemaic model, despite its mathematical sophistication, suffered from several conceptual and empirical shortcomings. One significant issue he identified was the reliance on epicycles and deferents—geometric constructs introduced to explain the irregular motions of the planets. While these devices allowed Ptolemy to achieve a degree of predictive accuracy, al-Razi maintained that they were ultimately artificial solutions that masked deeper inconsistencies within the system. By clinging to the notion of perfect circular motion, the Ptolemaic framework forced the universe into a contrived geometry that did not necessarily reflect the true nature of celestial phenomena.

The Problem of Empirical Discrepancies

Another major point of contention for al-Razi was the growing body of observational evidence that increasingly challenged the Ptolemaic paradigm. As astronomical techniques advanced, discrepancies between predicted and observed planetary positions became more pronounced. Al-Razi noted that the adjustments required by the Ptolemaic system to account for these deviations were not only cumbersome but also indicative of a fundamental flaw in its underlying assumptions. The need for successive corrections—each introducing additional layers of complexity—suggested that the geocentric model was not the natural order of the cosmos but a provisional construct in need of revision.

Philosophical and Theological Implications

Beyond its empirical shortcomings, the Ptolemaic system also carried significant philosophical and theological implications. By asserting that the Earth occupied a privileged, central position, the model implicitly elevated the status of the terrestrial over the celestial. Al-Razi found this anthropocentric bias problematic, arguing that it inadvertently reinforced a limited conception of the cosmos that confined divine grandeur to a narrow, Earth-bound perspective. For al-Razi, a truly comprehensive cosmology had to transcend the human scale and embrace a universe of boundless scope —a cosmos that reflected the infinite nature of its Creator.

In his critique, al-Razi called for a reimagining of the celestial order that would better accommodate both empirical observations and a more expansive theological vision. His doubts about the Ptolemaic system were not born out of mere contrarianism; rather, they emerged from a profound commitment to intellectual integrity and a desire to harmonize the insights of reason, observation, and divine revelation.

AL-RAZI'S ALTERNATIVE Cosmological Models (Mabahith al-Mashriqiyya)

A NEW VISION of the Cosmos

IN RESPONSE to the limitations he perceived in Ptolemaic astronomy, al-Razi advanced a series of alternative cosmological models that sought to capture the dynamic and intricate nature of the universe more faithfully. His work *Mabahith al-Mashriqiyya* represents a monumental effort to reconstruct cosmic theory along lines that integrated empirical observations with philosophical and theological insights. Al-Razi's models were characterized by their openness to complexity and their willingness to revise long-standing assumptions in light of new evidence.

MOVING Beyond a Fixed Center

ONE OF THE most revolutionary aspects of al-Razi's cosmological vision was his rejection of a fixed, central Earth. Instead of positioning the Earth as the immutable center of the universe, al-Razi envisaged a cosmos where the Earth was but one element in a vast, interconnected system. In his view, the universe was not a static edifice built around a central axis but a dynamic arena in which celestial bodies moved in intricate, interdependent patterns. This shift in perspective allowed for a more flexible and nuanced understanding of celestial motions—one that could accommodate irregularities without resorting to an ever-growing array of epicycles.

Embracing a Multiplicity of Worlds

Al-Razi's alternative models also ventured into the realm of what might be termed proto-multiverse theory. He speculated on the possibility that the universe might consist of multiple worlds or cosmic regions, each governed by its own set of physical laws and patterns of motion. Such a conception of the cosmos radically expanded the boundaries of astronomical thought, suggesting that the familiar night sky might be just a fraction of a far more complex and layered reality. In proposing these ideas, al-Razi anticipated later debates about the plurality of worlds—a topic that would gain renewed attention in subsequent centuries.

Integrating Observations with Metaphysical Principles

What sets al-Razi's models apart is their integration of meticulous observation with deep metaphysical inquiry. He was keenly aware that the cosmos, in all its vastness, could not be reduced solely to mechanical laws or mathematical formulas. Instead, he believed that the structure of the universe was imbued with purpose and meaning—a reflection of the divine order that permeated all creation. In *Mabahith al-Mashriqiyya*, al-Razi employed a dialectical method to reconcile empirical data with philosophical principles, arguing that the irregularities and complexities observed in celestial phenomena were not imperfections but signifiers of a deeper, metaphysical truth.

. . .

For example, al-Razi contended that the seemingly erratic motions of the planets could be understood as expressions of a cosmic harmony that transcended the rigid symmetry of circular orbits. He proposed that the variability in planetary speeds and directions might be the result of a more complex gravitational interplay—a precursor to ideas that would later evolve into modern theories of celestial mechanics. Through such insights, al-Razi demonstrated that a truly comprehensive cosmology must account for both the quantitative and qualitative aspects of the universe.

A Synthesis of Science and Spirituality

Perhaps the most enduring legacy of al-Razi's cosmological work is its synthesis of scientific inquiry with spiritual wisdom. His alternative models were not merely speculative exercises in astronomy; they were also deeply rooted in a theological vision of a universe that reflects the infinite creativity and wisdom of God. In al-Razi's thought, the cosmos is a living, dynamic tapestry—a manifestation of divine will that invites human beings to explore, question, and ultimately appreciate the sublime order of creation.

This integrative approach had profound implications for the development of later scientific and philosophical thought. By challenging the prevailing Ptolemaic paradigm and offering innovative alternatives, al-Razi opened the door to a more expansive and flexible understanding of the universe—one that would inspire subsequent generations of scholars to look beyond traditional boundaries and to embrace the complexity and mystery of cosmic order.

CONCLUSION

CHAPTER 9 HAS CHARTED a course through the evolving landscape of cosmological thought as seen through the eyes of al-Razi. His incisive critique of Ptolemaic astronomy laid bare the limitations of a geocentric model that, while mathematically elaborate, ultimately failed to capture the dynamic and interconnected nature of the cosmos. In its place, al-Razi proposed alternative cosmological models in *Mabahith al-Mashriqiyya* that not only accounted for empirical discrepancies but also integrated metaphysical and theological insights into a coherent vision of the universe.

BY DISCARDING the notion of a fixed center and entertaining the possibility of multiple worlds and intricate celestial interactions, al-Razi set the stage for a more fluid and comprehensive understanding of cosmic structure. His work remains a testament to the power of critical inquiry and the enduring human quest to decipher the mysteries of existence. In reconciling observation with spiritual wisdom, al-Razi offers a model of inquiry that continues to inspire, inviting us to view the cosmos not as a collection of isolated phenomena but as a vast, interwoven tapestry—a living reflection of divine order and creativity.

10
THE MULTIVERSE THEORY

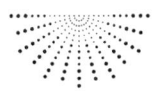

In this chapter, we venture into one of the most audacious and intellectually stimulating ideas in cosmological thought: the possibility that our universe is but one among many—a vast multiverse that transcends the limits of our conventional understanding. Al-Razi, ever the visionary, engaged with this concept long before it became a subject of modern scientific debate. His reflections on the multiverse challenge us to reconsider the boundaries of creation, the nature of cosmic order, and the role of divine providence in an ever-expanding tapestry of worlds.

Arguments for the Existence of Multiple Worlds

Reassessing the Limits of the Known Cosmos

The starting point of al-Razi's multiverse theory lies in his willingness to question the very boundaries of the observable universe. In his era, the cosmos was thought to be a singular, finite construct—one meticulously organized around the Earth or a central point of divine focus. However, al-Razi's rigorous inquiry into the structure of the universe led him to contemplate whether the cosmos might extend far beyond the limits imposed by traditional geocentric or even heliocentric models. He argued that if the universe displays such profound complexity and order, it may be unreasonable to assume that its totality is confined to the one world we directly perceive.

The Argument from Infinite Potentiality

One of the more striking lines of reasoning employed by al-Razi was the argument from infinite potentiality. He posited that if God is indeed the ultimate source of all creation, and if the divine nature is infinite, then it follows that the capacity for creation is boundless. Just as a master artist might produce countless variations on a theme, so too could the Creator fashion innumerable worlds, each governed by its own unique set of laws and characteristics. The idea here is not merely speculative; it is rooted in the notion that the divine attributes—such as omnipotence and eternal wisdom—necessitate a creation that is as vast and diverse as the nature of the Creator itself.

Empirical and Observational Hints

Although al-Razi's era did not have access to the advanced astronomical instruments of modern science, his meticulous observations of celestial phenomena led him to note irregularities and patterns that hinted at a broader, more intricate cosmic order. He observed that the motions and apparent configurations of stars and planets could not be fully explained by the Ptolemaic or early heliocentric models. Instead, he suggested that these anomalies might be interpreted as evidence of other cosmic realms—worlds that exist in parallel or in layered structures beyond our immediate perception. This argument from empirical hinting encourages a perspective where the observable universe is viewed as a fragment of a much larger, multifaceted reality.

The Logical Extension of Cosmological Principles

AL-RAZI'S REASONING further extended from the basic cosmological principle that every effect must have a cause, and every complex system must originate from simpler, generative processes. If the universe we observe is the product of such processes, then the same principles should, by logical extension, apply elsewhere. The formation of galaxies, stars, and planetary systems in our corner of the cosmos suggests that similar processes could be at work in other regions, creating discrete worlds with their own distinct properties. This argument is grounded in a rational extrapolation: if one part of creation is governed by a set of natural laws, then it is plausible to assume that these laws are universal in scope, allowing for the emergence of multiple worlds.

Theological and Philosophical Implications

Redefining the Notion of Creation

. . .

The theological implications of a multiverse are profound. For al-Razi, the recognition of multiple worlds serves to magnify the grandeur of divine creation. Instead of viewing the cosmos as a closed system centered on human experience, the multiverse theory expands the canvas of existence to include a plurality of realms—each reflecting a different facet of divine creativity. This expanded view not only reinforces the concept of God's boundless power and wisdom but also invites believers to appreciate the diversity of creation as a reflection of the infinite attributes of the Divine.

Reconciling Divine Immanence and Transcendence

The multiverse theory also offers an elegant solution to the perennial tension between divine immanence and transcendence. On one hand, the immanence of God is evident in the intimate involvement in the details of creation; on the other, divine transcendence implies that the Creator is beyond any single physical manifestation. By positing the existence of multiple worlds, al-Razi bridges this gap—suggesting that while God's presence permeates every aspect of the universe, the vastness of creation is such that no single world can encapsulate the totality of divine expression. This perspective elevates the notion of providence, presenting a vision where God is simultaneously immanent in every corner of existence and transcendent over an infinite expanse of worlds.

The Moral and Spiritual Dimensions

. . .

From a philosophical standpoint, the possibility of multiple worlds has far-reaching consequences for ethics and human self-understanding. If our universe is one among many, then the human quest for knowledge and moral improvement takes on a cosmic significance. The multiverse concept invites reflection on the uniqueness and interrelatedness of life across different realms. It challenges anthropocentric views by suggesting that the human experience, while central to our own world, is part of a larger tapestry of existence. Such a perspective can engender humility and wonder, reminding us that the moral order and spiritual purpose we seek might be part of a universal pattern—a design that extends far beyond our limited horizons.

Epistemological Expansion and the Limits of Human Knowledge

The introduction of multiple worlds into the framework of cosmology naturally leads to questions about the limits of human knowledge. Al-Razi's multiverse theory underscores the idea that the scope of our empirical investigations may be inherently constrained by our position within a singular world. The acknowledgment of a multiverse encourages scholars and seekers alike to embrace a posture of epistemological humility—recognizing that our current scientific and philosophical tools may only scratch the surface of a far more complex reality. This realization serves as both a challenge and an inspiration: a challenge to broaden our methods of inquiry and an inspiration to pursue knowledge with the awareness that each new discovery may reveal even greater mysteries.

. . .

A Catalyst for Interdisciplinary Dialogue

Finally, the multiverse theory stands as a catalyst for interdisciplinary dialogue between science, philosophy, and theology. Al-Razi's approach was never to confine cosmological speculation within the strict boundaries of any single discipline. Instead, he advocated for a synthesis of empirical observation, logical reasoning, and spiritual insight. In this light, the idea of multiple worlds becomes a point of convergence—a common ground where different modes of inquiry can interact fruitfully. Whether one is a scientist probing the mysteries of the cosmos, a philosopher grappling with the nature of existence, or a theologian seeking to understand the divine, the multiverse invites a collaborative quest for truth that transcends traditional disciplinary silos.

Conclusion

Chapter 10 has explored the bold and expansive notion of the multiverse as envisaged by al-Razi—a theory that challenges conventional cosmology and opens up new vistas of thought. Through a series of reasoned arguments, al-Razi advanced the possibility that the universe might be but one of many, each emerging from the inexhaustible wellspring of divine creativity. His arguments for the existence of multiple worlds rest on empirical observations, logical extrapolations, and a deep metaphysical commitment to the infinite nature of creation.

The theological and philosophical implications of this theory are equally transformative. The multiverse framework not only redefines our understanding of creation and divine action but also bridges the gap between immanence and transcendence, enriches our ethical and spiritual perspectives, and expands the horizons of human knowledge. In embracing the possibility of multiple worlds, al-Razi invites us to see the cosmos as a boundless, ever-unfolding tapestry—an intricate design that reflects the unfathomable wisdom and power of the Divine.

As we continue our exploration of cosmic and metaphysical mysteries, the multiverse theory stands as a testament to the enduring spirit of inquiry—a spirit that dares to challenge accepted paradigms and to envision a reality that is as infinite and multifaceted as the human imagination itself.

11
TIME AND SPACE

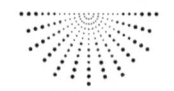

IN THIS CHAPTER, WE JOURNEY INTO THE PROFOUND REALMS OF time and space—two fundamental dimensions that underpin our understanding of the cosmos. Al-Razi, with his penetrating insight and willingness to challenge conventional wisdom, explored these topics with both scientific curiosity and metaphysical depth. He questioned whether time is eternal or created, whether space is finite or infinite, and offered unique views on the nature of the void. His reflections not only sought to reconcile empirical observation with philosophical inquiry but also to reveal a cosmos that is as dynamic and mysterious as it is ordered and purposeful.

The Nature of Time: Eternal or Created?

The Eternality of Time

ONE OF THE perennial questions in philosophy and theology is whether time itself is an eternal continuum or a phenomenon that was brought into existence at a specific moment. For al-Razi, the debate over the eternality of time is more than an abstract metaphysical puzzle—it is essential to understanding the very fabric of reality. He entertained the possibility that time might be eternal, an infinite dimension that has always flowed without a beginning or an end. This view resonates with the idea of an unchanging cosmic order, where time functions as the arena in which all events are interwoven, providing continuity and structure to the unfolding of creation.

In this eternal conception, time is not seen as a linear sequence starting with creation; instead, it is a perpetual backdrop against which the drama of existence plays out. Al-Razi suggested that if time were truly eternal, then the universe itself might be viewed as part of an infinite cycle of events, where the past and future are bound together in an endless recurrence. This perspective not only challenges the notion of a temporal beginning but also invites reflection on the nature of causality and change. How can events be meaningfully linked if time stretches back infinitely? Al-Razi addressed these concerns by proposing that the eternal nature of time need not contradict the existence of causality; rather, it offers a framework within which causal chains can extend indefinitely without diminishing their coherence.

Time as a Created Dimension

On the other side of the debate, al-Razi also considered the possibility that time is a created phenomenon—brought into being by a divine act and intricately linked to the moment of creation itself. In this view, time is not an independent, self-sustaining continuum but a contingent aspect of the cosmos, one that had its genesis alongside the physical universe. Here, time acquires a dual character: it is both a measure of change and a created order, imbued with meaning by the fact that it began at a specific point under divine will.

THIS CREATED model of time carries significant theological implications. If time had a beginning, then so did the universe, and this beginning becomes a point of convergence for scientific inquiry, philosophical speculation, and religious belief. It suggests that the unfolding of history—from the formation of galaxies to the evolution of life—is part of a purposeful design rather than an accidental occurrence. Al-Razi explored this perspective by emphasizing that a created time, marked by a definite starting point, enhances the notion of divine intervention in the world. It also raises questions about the nature of temporality: Does the creation of time imply that the future is open and contingent, while the past remains fixed? And how does this impact our understanding of destiny and free will? By grappling with these questions, al-Razi laid the groundwork for later debates in both philosophy and theology.

SYNTHESIS AND REFLECTION

IN CONTEMPLATING whether time is eternal or created, al-Razi did not insist on a definitive answer but rather celebrated the tension between these views. He proposed that both perspectives might capture different aspects of reality, suggesting that the divine nature could encompass both the unbounded continuity of time and its finite, measured expression within the created order. This synthesis invites us to see time as a multifaceted phenomenon—one that can be understood differently depending on the scale and context of inquiry. Ultimately, al-Razi's approach to time is one of openness and integration, recognizing that the mystery of time may never be fully resolved by human reason alone.

SPACE: Finite or Infinite?

THE CONCEPT of Finite Space

TURNING OUR ATTENTION TO SPACE, al-Razi confronted another age-old debate: Is space finite, confined within clear boundaries, or does it extend infinitely in all directions? In the finite model, space is seen as a bounded container, a well-defined arena within which all physical phenomena occur. This perspective is often linked with a universe that is ordered and measurable—a cosmos where every celestial body has its place and where the limits of existence can, in principle, be charted and understood.

AL-RAZI EXAMINED the finite view with a critical eye. He noted that if space were strictly finite, then the cosmos would have an outer limit—a boundary beyond which nothing exists. Such a boundary, however, poses significant philosophical and theological challenges. What lies beyond the confines of finite space? Would that boundary itself be subject to change, or would it represent an absolute, immutable limit? Al-Razi argued that while a finite space might offer a neat and comprehensible structure for the universe, it risks reducing the grandeur of creation to a mere geometrical construct. Moreover, the concept of a finite space raises questions about the nature of motion and the possibility of expansion or transformation within the cosmos.

The Argument for Infinite Space

Contrary to the finite model, the idea of infinite space envisions a cosmos that extends without limit—a boundless expanse where matter and energy are dispersed in an eternal continuum. For al-Razi, an infinite space is more consistent with the notion of a transcendent and omnipotent Creator, one whose power is not confined by any spatial limitations. In an infinite cosmos, every point is as significant as any other, and the diversity of creation is magnified by the sheer scale of existence.

Al-Razi found the concept of infinite space appealing because it allowed for a universe that is perpetually open to growth, change, and the emergence of new phenomena. It also aligns with his broader philosophical view that the divine is limitless. An infinite space, in this sense, becomes a metaphor for the infinite nature of God—a creation that mirrors the boundless attributes of its Creator. However, embracing infinite space also presents intellectual challenges. It forces us to confront the paradox of the infinite within a finite human understanding and to grapple with questions such as: How do we conceptualize the immeasurable? And can the human mind truly comprehend a cosmos without boundaries? Al-Razi's engagement with infinite space is a testament to his willingness to push the limits of conventional thought and to invite his contemporaries—and us—to ponder a reality that exceeds the ordinary.

Reconciling Finite and Infinite

IN HIS EXPLORATION OF SPACE, al-Razi did not simply advocate for one view over the other; he sought a nuanced understanding that could accommodate the strengths of both models. He suggested that space might possess a dual character: it could be finite in its observable and measurable aspects while simultaneously being infinite in its potential and underlying essence. Such a synthesis echoes his broader philosophical approach, which consistently emphasizes the interplay between the manifest and the transcendent. In this framework, the finite boundaries of space that we can chart are only a surface manifestation of a deeper, more expansive reality—a reality that is ultimately unbounded, like the divine itself.

Al-Razi's Views on the Void

Conceptualizing the Void

THE NOTION OF THE VOID—THE absence of matter or the emptiness that exists between celestial bodies—occupies a central place in al-Razi's cosmological vision. In his inquiry, the void is not seen as a mere vacuum devoid of significance but as a dynamic and integral part of the cosmic order. Al-Razi posited that the void plays a crucial role in the structure and behavior of the universe, serving as the stage upon which the drama of creation unfolds.

For al-Razi, the void is both a physical and metaphysical concept. Physically, it represents the spaces between stars, planets, and galaxies—the expanses that appear empty to the naked eye yet are permeated by subtle forces and energies. Metaphysically, the void symbolizes the potentiality of creation, the unmanifest that lies beyond the visible and the measurable. It is a reminder that the absence of matter is not equivalent to the absence of being, but rather a state of latent possibility from which new forms and structures may emerge.

The Role of the Void in Cosmic Dynamics

Al-Razi was particularly interested in how the void interacts with the matter that occupies space. He argued that the void is essential for allowing motion and change within the cosmos. Without the empty spaces between objects, the dynamic processes of creation—such as the movement of planets, the expansion of the universe, and the transmission of energy—would be impossible. The void, therefore, is not a passive backdrop but an active component in the orchestration of cosmic phenomena.

Moreover, al-Razi saw the void as a symbol of the interplay between absence and presence—a duality that is fundamental to his understanding of the universe. The tension between the void and the filled space mirrors the broader dialectic between the finite and the infinite, the created and the eternal. In contemplating the void, al-Razi invites us to reflect on the paradoxical nature of existence: that within the emptiness there lies the seed of potential, and that what appears to be nothingness may, in fact, be the wellspring of all being.

. . .

PHILOSOPHICAL AND THEOLOGICAL **Significance**

THE EXPLORATION of the void carries profound philosophical and theological implications. By affirming that the void is an indispensable element of the cosmos, al-Razi challenges the simplistic notion that emptiness is synonymous with non-existence. Instead, he posits that the void is a necessary condition for the unfolding of the divine plan—a space where the forces of creation can be mobilized and new realities can be forged.

THIS VIEW of the void reinforces the idea that the universe is a harmonious interplay of opposites: light and darkness, fullness and emptiness, being and non-being. It is a perspective that resonates with many mystical traditions, which see the void not as a nihilistic absence but as a fertile ground for spiritual and cosmic regeneration. In this light, al-Razi's reflections on the void offer a powerful metaphor for the transformative potential inherent in every gap and hiatus in the tapestry of existence.

CONCLUSION

CHAPTER 11 HAS NAVIGATED the intricate landscapes of time and space through the lens of al-Razi's thought, challenging us to rethink the dimensions that govern our reality. We have examined the dual nature of time—whether it is an eternal continuum or a created phenomenon—each perspective offering profound insights into the nature of causality, change, and divine action. In parallel, we have explored the debate over the finitude or infinitude of space, considering both the measurable boundaries of the cosmos and the limitless potential that lies beyond them.

Central to this inquiry is al-Razi's innovative view of the void—a concept that transcends the mere absence of matter to embody the latent possibility inherent in every gap of existence. By engaging with these themes, al-Razi not only advanced a sophisticated cosmological vision but also invited a dialogue that bridges empirical observation with philosophical and theological reflection.

In embracing the complexities of time and space, al-Razi's work continues to inspire us to explore the vast, interwoven tapestry of the cosmos—a realm where the known and the mysterious converge, and where every moment and every measure of space is a testament to the infinite creativity of the Divine.

12
THE NATURE OF THE SOUL

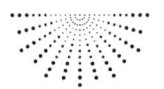

In this chapter, we embark on an in-depth exploration of the soul—its essence, its immortality, and its intricate relationship with the body. Drawing on the profound insights of al-Razi, we examine the soul not merely as an abstract concept but as the vibrant, dynamic core of human existence. This inquiry into the nature of the soul interweaves metaphysical inquiry with empirical reflection, seeking to reveal a vision of the self that is both transcendent and intimately connected to the physical world.

The Soul's Essence and Immortality

The Essence of the Soul

Al-Razi approached the soul with an acute sensitivity to its multifaceted nature. He viewed the soul as the defining attribute that distinguishes living beings from inanimate matter—a subtle, non-material principle that animates the body and enables cognition, emotion, and spiritual aspiration. Far from being a mere byproduct of bodily processes, the soul, in al-Razi's perspective, is the repository of reason, memory, and the capacity for moral judgment. It is the seat of consciousness, the spark of intellect that allows human beings to engage with both the visible and invisible realms.

IN HIS WRITINGS, al-Razi emphasizes that the soul is inherently self-reflective and capable of introspection. This quality enables individuals to pursue knowledge, to contemplate ethical principles, and to seek a connection with the divine. The soul's essence, therefore, is not static; it is characterized by an ever-present potential for growth and transformation. It is through the cultivation of the soul—via intellectual inquiry, spiritual practices, and ethical refinement—that one can move closer to a fuller understanding of truth and reality.

The Immortality of the Soul

ONE OF THE most enduring questions in philosophy is whether the soul is subject to decay or whether it persists beyond the limits of mortal life. Al-Razi was a vigorous proponent of the soul's immortality. For him, the soul was not bound by the same limitations as the physical body; rather, it was an eternal entity that survives the vicissitudes of earthly existence. This view of immortality is not grounded solely in speculative metaphysics but is deeply interwoven with the theological vision that sees human life as part of a larger cosmic narrative.

. . .

ACCORDING TO AL-RAZI, the soul's immortality is essential for understanding the moral and intellectual dimensions of human life. If the soul were to perish with the body, then the pursuit of wisdom, the exercise of virtue, and the accountability for one's actions would be rendered ultimately meaningless. Immortality, by contrast, provides the basis for an ongoing journey of self-improvement and spiritual evolution —a journey that extends beyond the temporal constraints of physical existence.

AL-RAZI ALSO SAW the immortality of the soul as a vindication of the higher truths revealed through divine revelation. The eternal nature of the soul reinforces the idea that there exists a reality beyond the transient world of sensory experience—a reality that is accessible through both rational inquiry and spiritual insight. In this framework, the soul serves as the bridge between the finite human condition and the infinite, unchanging nature of the divine.

The Relationship Between Soul and Body

The Dual Nature of Human Existence

CENTRAL TO AL-RAZI'S thought is the recognition of a dual aspect of human existence: the union of body and soul. While the body is the tangible, material component that interacts with the external world, the soul represents the immaterial core that defines personal identity and consciousness. This duality is not viewed in terms of opposition, but rather as a complementary relationship in which each element contributes to the full realization of human potential.

AL-RAZI ARGUED that the body serves as the vessel through which the soul expresses its intellectual and moral capacities. It is the physical interface with the world—a channel for sensory experience, emotional engagement, and social interaction. However, the body is inherently limited by its material nature; it is subject to decay, pain, and the vicissitudes of physical change. The soul, by contrast, is the enduring principle that gives life its purpose and continuity. It is the source of creativity, the engine of reason, and the wellspring of spiritual insight.

THE INTERDEPENDENCE of Body and Soul

RATHER THAN POSITING a strict separation between the soul and the body, al-Razi maintained that their relationship is fundamentally interdependent. The health and vitality of the soul can be nurtured or impaired by the state of the body, just as the body is animated and directed by the soul. For example, the practice of ethical behavior, intellectual exercise, and spiritual meditation can have beneficial effects on physical well-being, while neglect or corruption of the soul may manifest in physical malaise.

THIS INTERDEPENDENCE also has profound implications for the understanding of human experience. Al-Razi observed that while the body is susceptible to suffering and limitation, the soul retains the capacity to transcend these conditions through contemplation, moral striving, and the pursuit of higher knowledge. In times of physical adversity, the soul can offer solace and strength; conversely, a body that is nurtured and cared for provides a stable environment in which the soul can flourish. This symbiotic relationship underscores the holistic nature of human existence, where the material and immaterial are in constant dialogue.

Philosophical Reflections on the Unity of Self

AL-RAZI'S INSIGHTS into the soul-body relationship further lead to a nuanced conception of personal identity. He posited that the true self is not reducible solely to the physical or to the spiritual but is a unified whole that emerges from their synthesis. This unity is the basis of individual identity, continuity over time, and the capacity for self-determination. It is the harmonious interaction of body and soul that enables a person to act, to love, and to seek truth.

MOREOVER, this unity challenges the often reductionist views that attempt to diminish the soul to mere biological or psychological processes. Instead, al-Razi's vision affirms the soul as a distinct, immortal essence that interacts with the body in a dynamic and meaningful way. In this light, the human being is seen as a microcosm of the cosmic order—a living embodiment of the eternal principles that govern the universe.

Ethical and Spiritual Implications

. . .

The intricate interplay between soul and body has significant ethical and spiritual implications. Al-Razi's perspective encourages a holistic approach to self-improvement, one that recognizes the importance of nurturing both the physical and the spiritual dimensions of life. This approach calls for a balanced lifestyle—one that integrates physical health, intellectual cultivation, and spiritual practice. It is through the harmonious development of both aspects that one can achieve true fulfillment and contribute meaningfully to the world.

Furthermore, the recognition of the soul's immortality and its inseparable link to the body provides a robust framework for understanding moral responsibility. Since the soul endures beyond physical death, the choices made in this life carry an eternal weight. This insight fosters a deep sense of accountability and a commitment to the cultivation of virtue, as the well-being of the soul is paramount to the realization of a truly meaningful existence.

Conclusion

Chapter 12 has explored the profound nature of the soul through the dual lenses of its essence and its relationship with the body. Al-Razi's insights illuminate the soul as the enduring, dynamic core of human existence—an entity that transcends the limitations of the physical while engaging intimately with the material world. By affirming the soul's capacity for immortality, al-Razi establishes a basis for moral responsibility, intellectual pursuit, and spiritual growth that extends beyond the confines of mortal life.

. . .

The relationship between the soul and the body, as conceived by al-Razi, is one of mutual enrichment and interdependence. Far from being antagonistic forces, they combine to form the complete human being—a unity that reflects both the transient beauty of the physical world and the eternal radiance of the divine. This holistic vision not only offers a deep understanding of personal identity but also invites us to nurture every facet of our existence in the quest for truth, wisdom, and ultimate fulfillment.

In engaging with these themes, we are reminded that the journey of self-discovery is as much about honoring the imperishable light of the soul as it is about caring for the vessel through which that light shines. Al-Razi's reflections thus continue to inspire, challenging us to strive for a balance between our earthly experiences and our transcendent aspirations—a balance that lies at the heart of what it means to be truly human.

13
KNOWLEDGE AND THE SOUL

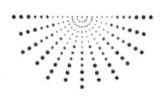

In this chapter, we explore the profound interplay between the soul and the pursuit of knowledge—a relationship that al-Razi considered central to the human experience and the quest for intellectual perfection. By examining the soul's capacity for knowledge and its ultimate role in achieving intellectual and spiritual fulfillment, we gain insight into a vision of the self that extends beyond mere sensory perception into the realm of eternal wisdom. Al-Razi's perspective on these themes weaves together elements of metaphysics, epistemology, and theology, ultimately presenting a model of human existence in which the cultivation of knowledge is both a worldly endeavor and a pathway to the transcendent.

The Soul's Capacity for Knowledge

The Innate Intellectual Faculty

For al-Razi, the soul is far more than the source of life or consciousness—it is the wellspring of intellectual potential. He maintained that every human being is endowed with an inherent capacity for knowledge, a divine spark that enables the mind to perceive, reflect, and understand the multifaceted nature of reality. This intellectual faculty is not acquired solely through external education or sensory experience but is intrinsic to the very nature of the soul. It empowers individuals to engage with abstract concepts, to unravel the complexities of nature, and to contemplate both the physical and metaphysical dimensions of existence.

The Process of Intellectual Illumination

Al-Razi believed that the journey toward knowledge is a process of illumination in which the soul gradually frees itself from the shadows of ignorance. This process involves a combination of empirical observation, rational analysis, and introspective reflection. The soul, as it encounters the truths of the world, experiences moments of clarity that not only enhance its understanding but also uplift it to higher levels of consciousness. Such moments of intellectual illumination are seen as gifts of divine grace—instances when the barriers between the finite and the infinite momentarily dissolve, allowing the soul to apprehend deeper truths.

The Role of Contemplation and Reflection

Central to harnessing the soul's capacity for knowledge is the practice of contemplation. Al-Razi emphasized that the pursuit of wisdom requires more than just the accumulation of facts; it demands a reflective engagement with those facts. Contemplation is the process through which the soul distills the essence of experience and transforms raw information into meaningful insights. This reflective state not only nurtures intellectual growth but also aligns the individual with a higher, universal order. In this light, the cultivation of knowledge is both a personal and a spiritual discipline—one that requires patience, humility, and an unyielding commitment to truth.

The Interplay of Reason and Revelation

While empirical investigation and logical reasoning are indispensable to the acquisition of knowledge, al-Razi also recognized the vital role of revelation in guiding the soul. Divine revelation, transmitted through sacred texts and prophetic teachings, offers insights that complement and even surpass the capabilities of human reason. For al-Razi, the soul's quest for knowledge reaches its fullest expression when it harmonizes the insights gained from reason with the profound truths revealed by the divine. This synthesis of rational inquiry and spiritual illumination creates a holistic epistemology, one in which the pursuit of knowledge is elevated to a sacred duty—a means of transcending the limitations of the material world and touching the eternal.

Intellectual Perfection and the Afterlife

The Concept of Intellectual Perfection

. . .

INTELLECTUAL PERFECTION, for al-Razi, represents the highest form of human fulfillment. It is an ideal state in which the soul has achieved a comprehensive understanding of both the natural and metaphysical worlds. This perfection is not merely the accumulation of knowledge but the transformation of the self into a vessel of wisdom and virtue. It implies a harmonious alignment between the intellectual and moral dimensions of the individual—where critical insight and ethical conduct are mutually reinforcing.

ACHIEVING intellectual perfection is seen as an ongoing journey rather than a fixed destination. It involves the continuous refinement of thought, the diligent pursuit of truth, and the willingness to question and reexamine one's beliefs. For al-Razi, this perpetual quest for knowledge is both a personal and communal endeavor, one that enriches not only the individual soul but also the broader tapestry of human civilization. In reaching toward intellectual perfection, the soul transcends the limitations imposed by ignorance and error, evolving into an instrument capable of discerning the subtle interplay between cause and effect, order and chaos, the finite and the infinite.

THE AFTERLIFE as the Realm of Intellectual Fulfillment

THE CONCEPT of the afterlife plays a pivotal role in al-Razi's vision of intellectual perfection. He posited that the pursuit of knowledge does not end with mortal life but continues into the realm of the eternal. In the afterlife, the soul—unencumbered by the distractions and limitations of the physical body—can attain a level of intellectual clarity and spiritual insight that remains elusive in the temporal world. This state of perfection is not a mere reward but the natural culmination of a life dedicated to the pursuit of truth.

AL-RAZI'S VIEW of the afterlife is deeply intertwined with the moral and intellectual progress achieved during earthly existence. The choices made by an individual in life, the cultivation of wisdom, and the adherence to ethical principles all contribute to the state of the soul after death. In this sense, intellectual perfection is both a goal and a means of attaining eternal fulfillment. The afterlife becomes a realm where the soul can finally engage in the pure contemplation of divine truths, free from the distortions of physical reality—a state in which the intellect reaches its ultimate expression and the mysteries of existence are laid bare.

THE TRANSFORMATION of the Soul

THE JOURNEY toward intellectual perfection is transformative. As the soul accumulates knowledge and refines its understanding, it undergoes a metamorphosis that reshapes its very essence. This transformation is marked by a gradual detachment from the ephemeral and a deepening engagement with the eternal. Through this process, the soul not only becomes a repository of wisdom but also an active participant in the unfolding of divine purpose. The transformation is both internal and external: internally, it manifests as a profound shift in consciousness and character; externally, it influences the way an individual interacts with the world, inspiring actions that are aligned with higher ideals.

. . .

THIS TRANSFORMATIVE JOURNEY has significant implications for the concept of the afterlife. The more the soul perfects its intellect, the more prepared it is to enter into the eternal realm where intellectual and spiritual rewards await. In this context, intellectual perfection is seen not as an end in itself but as a vital stage in the soul's ongoing evolution—a necessary preparation for the ultimate encounter with the divine.

THE SYNERGY OF KNOWLEDGE, Virtue, and Immortality

AL-RAZI'S EXPLORATION of the relationship between knowledge and the soul is deeply rooted in the idea that true intellectual achievement must be accompanied by ethical refinement. Knowledge, when divorced from virtue, can lead to arrogance, misguidance, or even moral decay. Conversely, the pursuit of wisdom that is grounded in ethical principles produces a synergy between the mind and the heart—a unity that enhances both intellectual clarity and moral responsibility.

IN THIS SYNERGISTIC MODEL, the attainment of knowledge becomes inseparable from the cultivation of virtue, and intellectual perfection is seen as the harmonious balance of these two dimensions. The soul, by nurturing both its cognitive faculties and its ethical sensibilities, prepares itself for an existence that is not only enlightened but also eternally fulfilling. This balanced approach ensures that the quest for knowledge is directed toward the ultimate good—a good that transcends individual achievement and contributes to the collective well-being of humanity.

. . .

Conclusion

Chapter 13 has navigated the intricate terrain of the soul's relationship with knowledge, revealing a vision in which intellectual inquiry is both a personal odyssey and a pathway to eternal fulfillment. Al-Razi's insights illuminate the profound capacity of the soul to engage with and absorb knowledge—a capacity that is intrinsic to human nature and reflective of the divine spark within. Through the process of contemplation, the interplay of reason and revelation, and the transformative journey toward intellectual perfection, the soul is elevated from the mundane to the sublime.

Furthermore, al-Razi's conception of intellectual perfection as a precursor to a transcendent afterlife underscores the idea that the pursuit of knowledge is not confined to the temporal realm. Instead, it is an enduring commitment that shapes the destiny of the soul, preparing it for a state of eternal clarity and communion with the divine. In this synthesis of knowledge, virtue, and immortality, al-Razi offers a compelling model of human potential—one that challenges us to embrace the pursuit of wisdom as a lifelong, transformative journey.

As we reflect on these themes, we are invited to see our own intellectual and spiritual endeavors as part of a grand, cosmic tapestry—a tapestry in which every moment of insight, every act of reflection, and every step toward ethical perfection contributes to the everlasting evolution of the soul.

14
THE AFTERLIFE AND ESCHATOLOGY

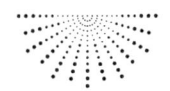

In this final chapter, we explore the profound and enduring questions of the afterlife and eschatology—the study of final events in human history. For al-Razi, these themes are not remote speculations but core elements of a cosmology that connects the temporal world with eternal realities. Through his critical engagement with doctrines of resurrection, judgment, and the nature of paradise and hell, as elaborated in works such as *Mafatih al-Ghayb*, al-Razi invites us to reconsider what it means to live, die, and ultimately be held accountable in a grand cosmic drama.

Resurrection and Judgment

The Concept of Resurrection

Al-Razi's examination of resurrection begins with the understanding that life does not cease with death; instead, the soul embarks on a journey that culminates in a reawakening—a return to a state of existence that transcends the limitations of the earthly body. Resurrection, in his view, is the ultimate vindication of the soul's immortality. It is not a mere revival of the physical form but a transformative event in which the soul, purified through its earthly experiences, is reunited with a body that has been sanctified by divine will.

THIS PROCESS IS IMBUED with profound symbolism. It represents the triumph of order over decay, of eternal truth over temporal existence. The resurrection is seen as a necessary step in the cosmic order, providing a resolution to the apparent finality of death. In al-Razi's framework, the resurrection is also a metaphysical affirmation that the material and immaterial are destined to converge—where the impermanent flesh gives way to an enduring form that is capable of experiencing the full range of divine justice and mercy.

THE DAY of Judgment

CLOSELY LINKED to the concept of resurrection is the doctrine of judgment. Al-Razi posits that following the resurrection, all souls will face an incontrovertible judgment —an event of cosmic significance where every individual is held accountable for their thoughts, actions, and the cultivation of wisdom during their earthly life. This judgment is not arbitrary; it is grounded in the principles of divine justice and mercy.

FOR AL-RAZI, judgment serves several critical functions:
- **Moral Accountability:** It reinforces the idea that ethical conduct and the pursuit of knowledge are paramount. Every

action contributes to the moral ledger that determines one's eternal destiny.

- **Cosmic Order:** It restores balance in the universe, affirming that every cause has its effect. The process of judgment aligns with the rational order of creation, where every deed is measured against the immutable standards of truth.
- **Spiritual Purification:** Judgment is also seen as a purgative process. It not only distinguishes the righteous from the unrighteous but also cleanses the soul, preparing it for its eventual union with the divine.

AL-RAZI'S VISION of judgment is marked by its rigorous yet compassionate nature. While the criteria are exacting, the ultimate purpose is to facilitate the soul's journey toward perfection. The accountability that accompanies judgment is not a cause for despair but a call to conscientious living—a reminder that the pursuit of truth and virtue shapes one's eternal fate.

PARADISE AND HELL: Literal or Metaphorical? (Mafatih al-Ghayb)

THE NATURE of Paradise

IN HIS SEMINAL work *Mafatih al-Ghayb*, al-Razi delves into the descriptions of paradise, challenging readers to consider whether these portrayals are to be understood literally or metaphorically. Paradise, in the eschatological vision, is traditionally depicted as a realm of unimaginable beauty and eternal bliss—a reward for the virtuous and the wise. Al-Razi acknowledges the conventional imagery of lush gardens, flowing rivers, and radiant mansions but urges a deeper reflection on their significance.

For al-Razi, the descriptions of paradise can be seen on two levels:
• **Literal Dimensions:** At face value, the detailed accounts of paradise provide a concrete vision of what awaits the soul—a place of physical delight where every need is abundantly met. This literal interpretation has the merit of inspiring hope and moral discipline by presenting a tangible goal.
• **Metaphorical Dimensions:** On a more profound level, however, paradise serves as a powerful metaphor for the state of intellectual and spiritual perfection. In this reading, the vivid imagery symbolizes the ultimate realization of the soul's potential—the attainment of a harmonious, unblemished state of being where all the illusions of the material world are dispelled. Paradise becomes the emblem of a mind liberated from ignorance, an existence marked by the presence of divine wisdom and moral clarity.

The Nature of Hell

The concept of hell, as with paradise, is a subject of intense scrutiny in al-Razi's thought. Traditionally portrayed as a realm of suffering and torment—a punishment for the wicked—hell is presented in stark contrast to the bliss of paradise. Al-Razi, however, is careful not to reduce these descriptions to mere retributive imagery. He sees them as expressions of the profound consequences that follow from the neglect of truth and virtue.
• **Literal Interpretation:** On one level, the graphic depic-

tions of hell serve as a deterrent against moral and intellectual complacency. They underscore the reality that a life devoid of ethical reflection and the pursuit of knowledge carries with it dire consequences. The pain and despair described in these accounts are not gratuitous; they symbolize the loss of opportunity to engage with the highest truths.

- **Metaphorical Interpretation:** Beyond the literal, hell can be understood metaphorically as the state of spiritual alienation and intellectual stagnation. It represents a condition where the soul is mired in the darkness of ignorance and moral decay. In this metaphorical reading, the torments of hell are not inflicted by an external force but are the natural outcome of a self-imposed separation from the divine. Such a state is marked by an inner desolation—a life bereft of hope, purpose, and the guiding light of wisdom.

BRIDGING the Dual Interpretations

AL-RAZI'S TREATMENT of paradise and hell in *Mafatih al-Ghayb* reflects his broader epistemological and theological method: an insistence on the coexistence of literal and metaphorical truths. He contends that while the descriptions of the afterlife can be approached as concrete realities, they simultaneously function as symbols that encapsulate the moral and intellectual trajectories of human life. In his view, the afterlife is not merely an arena of physical rewards and punishments but a continuum of existential states that mirror the soul's journey toward or away from divine truth.

BY ACKNOWLEDGING THE DUAL INTERPRETATIONS, al-Razi invites us to appreciate the eschatological visions as multilayered narratives. They are at once promises of hope for the righteous and warnings to the heedless, crafted in a language that speaks to both the corporeal and the transcendent dimensions of human experience. This layered approach ensures that the eschatological discourse remains relevant and compelling, providing a framework for understanding both the external consequences of one's actions and the internal evolution of the self.

Conclusion

Chapter 14 has taken us deep into the realms of the afterlife and eschatology as envisaged by al-Razi—a vision where resurrection, judgment, paradise, and hell are not isolated doctrines but interconnected elements of a grand cosmic order. His exploration of resurrection and judgment emphasizes the eternal accountability of the soul, where every act and intention is measured against the immutable standards of divine justice. This process, far from being punitive, is designed to purify and elevate the soul, preparing it for a reunion with the eternal.

At the same time, al-Razi's nuanced treatment of paradise and hell—as articulated in *Mafatih al-Ghayb*—challenges us to look beyond literal depictions. These realms are imbued with symbolic significance, representing the ultimate outcomes of intellectual and moral endeavors. Paradise stands as the embodiment of a perfected soul—a state of unblemished enlightenment and spiritual harmony—while hell symbolizes the tragic consequences of turning away from truth and virtue, a descent into the void of ignorance and despair.

. . .

IN EMBRACING both the literal and metaphorical dimensions of these eschatological concepts, al-Razi not only deepens our understanding of the afterlife but also reinforces the enduring relevance of moral and intellectual striving in our lives. The vision he offers is one where every choice, every pursuit of knowledge, and every act of virtue contributes to the soul's eternal destiny. It is an invitation to live in a manner that recognizes the profound interconnectedness of earthly existence and the eternal, urging us to cultivate wisdom, embrace moral responsibility, and ultimately prepare for the grand culmination of our journey—a reunion with the divine in the boundless realms of eternity.

15
THE FOUNDATIONS OF ETHICS

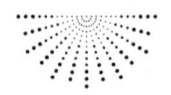

In this chapter, we turn our attention to one of the most enduring and universal areas of inquiry—the nature of ethics. Grounded in the rich intellectual tradition of al-Razi, this exploration seeks to understand the very essence of good and evil, the basis for moral responsibility, and the role of divine justice in shaping human conduct. Rather than treating ethics as a mere set of abstract rules, al-Razi's approach reveals it as an integrated framework that underpins both individual character and the cosmic order. Through rigorous reasoning and reflective insight, this chapter unfolds the multilayered dimensions of ethical thought, inviting us to consider how our actions, intentions, and choices contribute to the moral fabric of existence.

The Nature of Good and Evil

Defining Good and Evil

. . .

At the heart of ethical inquiry lies the challenge of defining what constitutes good and what falls under the realm of evil. For al-Razi, good is not simply a relative or culturally determined standard; it is grounded in the inherent order of the universe—a reflection of divine wisdom and the natural law that governs all creation. Good, in this framework, is associated with qualities such as harmony, balance, and the flourishing of life. It is the principle that aligns with the universal order and promotes the well-being of the individual, society, and creation itself.

Evil, by contrast, is understood as a deviation from this natural order—a disruption that causes imbalance, suffering, or moral decay. It is not merely the absence of good, but often an active force that undermines the conditions for a harmonious existence. Al-Razi posited that while the definitions of good and evil may sometimes appear contingent on specific circumstances, they ultimately point toward immutable truths that are rooted in the divine order of the cosmos.

The Duality and Interdependence of Opposites

Al-Razi's exploration of good and evil also emphasizes the dynamic interplay between opposites. Drawing on a dialectical method, he suggests that the contrast between these forces is essential for understanding their nature. Just as light is defined by the presence of darkness, good and evil serve as complementary aspects of a broader ethical spectrum. This duality is not meant to establish a simplistic binary; rather, it encourages a nuanced view in which moments of moral ambiguity and conflict serve as opportunities for growth and self-refinement.

IN THIS DIALECTICAL PERSPECTIVE, the existence of evil provides the context in which the virtues of good can shine forth. It is through confronting and overcoming challenges that individuals are able to cultivate moral strength, develop resilience, and deepen their understanding of ethical principles. Consequently, the struggle between good and evil is seen not only as a source of conflict but also as a catalyst for moral evolution and personal transformation.

THE ROLE of Reason in Ethical Judgement

FOR AL-RAZI, the capacity for ethical judgment is deeply intertwined with the rational faculties of the soul. Reason plays a pivotal role in discerning the nuances between right and wrong. By engaging in critical reflection and thoughtful deliberation, individuals can identify the underlying principles that define moral action. This rational approach does not diminish the emotional and intuitive dimensions of ethics; instead, it complements them by providing a structured framework within which moral values can be examined, articulated, and justified.

IN THIS LIGHT, the pursuit of ethics is both a cognitive and a moral endeavor. It demands not only the cultivation of intellectual clarity but also the exercise of virtues such as humility, empathy, and integrity. Through the balanced application of reason and emotion, one is able to navigate the complexities of ethical decision-making and strive toward a life that is both morally consistent and deeply fulfilling.

Moral Responsibility and Divine Justice

The Burden of Moral Responsibility

A CENTRAL TENET of al-Razi's ethical framework is the idea that human beings are endowed with moral responsibility—a capacity that arises from the inherent dignity and rationality of the soul. This responsibility is not arbitrary or externally imposed; it is a natural consequence of our ability to understand, reflect upon, and shape our actions according to universal ethical principles. Every decision, every act, carries with it the weight of accountability. This moral responsibility extends beyond individual conduct; it influences the character of communities and, ultimately, the order of society as a whole.

AL-RAZI CONTENDS that the exercise of moral responsibility is what elevates human existence. It is through responsible action that individuals contribute to the collective well-being and participate in the ongoing work of creation. When individuals choose to align their actions with the principles of good, they affirm their role as active co-creators of a harmonious world. Conversely, when one neglects or misuses this freedom, the resultant dissonance reverberates not only on a personal level but also across the broader fabric of society.

Divine Justice as the Ultimate Arbiter

. . .

Central to the ethical vision of al-Razi is the concept of divine justice—a principle that underpins the moral order of the universe. Divine justice is not merely a mechanism of retribution; it is an expression of the perfect, all-encompassing wisdom that governs creation. In al-Razi's thought, every act of moral responsibility is ultimately accountable to a higher authority—a divine judge whose wisdom transcends human limitations. This understanding of justice provides a framework within which every individual is seen as an integral part of a larger cosmic narrative, where moral deeds are recorded, and every choice has eternal significance.

Divine justice functions as both a corrective and a guiding force. It ensures that the scales of moral balance are maintained, rewarding acts that contribute to the common good while addressing those that disrupt the natural order. Yet, divine justice is tempered with mercy, reflecting the compassion and understanding that are as much a part of the divine nature as are truth and fairness. This balanced conception of justice offers hope and accountability in equal measure, reminding individuals that ethical conduct has far-reaching implications that extend beyond immediate circumstances.

The Interconnection of Ethics, Free Will, and Accountability

Al-Razi's ethical framework intricately weaves together the ideas of free will, moral responsibility, and divine justice. Human freedom is the foundation upon which ethical accountability is built. The capacity to choose is what distinguishes human beings from mere automatons, enabling us to engage in meaningful ethical deliberation. With this freedom comes the duty to exercise it wisely—a duty that is reinforced by the understanding that our choices have eternal consequences.

By emphasizing the interplay between free will and accountability, al-Razi underscores the transformative potential of ethical action. When individuals act in accordance with their highest values, they participate in a self-affirming process that reinforces their dignity and propels them toward moral and intellectual perfection. At the same time, the awareness of divine justice acts as a safeguard against moral complacency, encouraging a conscientious and deliberate approach to life that honors both the individual and the greater cosmic order.

The Ethical Implications for Society

The implications of al-Razi's ethical vision extend far beyond the individual. A society that embraces the principles of moral responsibility and divine justice is one that nurtures ethical behavior on all levels. Such a society is characterized by mutual respect, compassion, and a commitment to the common good—a community in which every member is valued not only for their personal virtues but also for their contribution to the collective moral fabric.

In practical terms, this ethical framework calls for institutions and practices that reinforce accountability, promote justice, and cultivate virtue. Education, for example, becomes not merely a means of acquiring knowledge but a vital process for instilling moral values and encouraging ethical reflection. Similarly, systems of governance and law are seen as extensions of the divine order, tasked with maintaining social harmony and ensuring that justice is administered with both firmness and fairness.

Conclusion

Chapter 15 has taken us on a comprehensive journey through the foundational dimensions of ethics as envisioned by al-Razi. At its core, this exploration reveals that ethics is not a set of isolated principles but a dynamic and interrelated system that defines the nature of good and evil, underpins moral responsibility, and is anchored in the overarching concept of divine justice.

The nature of good and evil, as discussed in this chapter, is deeply intertwined with the universal order—reflecting the harmony or discord that results from our actions. By understanding that good aligns with the intrinsic order of creation and that evil represents a deviation from this order, we are called to a heightened awareness of our moral duties. In turn, moral responsibility emerges as an essential attribute of human existence—one that demands both intellectual reflection and the practical exercise of free will.

Divine justice, in al-Razi's view, is the ultimate arbiter that binds individual accountability to the cosmic scale of morality. It offers both retribution and mercy, ensuring that every act contributes to a balanced and meaningful order. This integrated vision of ethics not only elevates personal conduct but also lays the groundwork for a just and compassionate society.

IN EMBRACING THESE ETHICAL FOUNDATIONS, al-Razi invites us to engage in a lifelong commitment to truth, virtue, and justice. The quest for moral perfection is not merely an abstract ideal; it is a practical, transformative journey that enriches the soul, nurtures the community, and aligns human action with the eternal principles that govern the universe. As we reflect on these teachings, we are reminded that every ethical choice contributes to the unfolding of a grand, cosmic tapestry—one that is ultimately woven by the divine hand of justice and compassion.

16
VIRTUES AND VICES

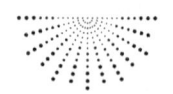

IN THIS CHAPTER, WE EMBARK ON AN IN-DEPTH EXPLORATION of the ethical terrain defined by virtues and vices—a dual framework that has long served as the foundation for moral inquiry. Drawing on the rich tradition of Islamic thought, al-Razi's reflections guide us through the cardinal virtues and the pitfalls of vice, inviting us to cultivate moral excellence and avoid the traps that lead to ethical decay. This chapter unfolds in two parts: first, we delve into the cardinal virtues as understood within the Islamic intellectual heritage; then, we explore practical strategies for moral improvement—a roadmap for transforming character and fostering a life of virtue.

The Cardinal Virtues in Islamic Thought

The Heritage of Virtue

. . .

In the Islamic ethical tradition, virtues are seen not as abstract ideals but as practical habits that shape both individual character and communal well-being. Rooted in the Quran, the teachings of the Prophet, and the intellectual contributions of scholars like al-Razi, the cardinal virtues provide a comprehensive framework for understanding what it means to lead a morally upright life. These virtues are seen as the natural expressions of divine wisdom—a reflection of the Creator's own attributes manifested in the human soul.

Core Virtues Defined

Among the many virtues extolled in Islamic thought, a handful are considered cardinal because they underpin all other moral qualities. These include:

- **Wisdom (Hikmah):** Recognized as the guiding light of human action, wisdom in Islamic thought involves both intellectual insight and practical judgment. It is not merely knowledge for its own sake, but the discernment to act rightly in the face of life's complexities. For al-Razi, wisdom is essential to align the human mind with divine order, enabling individuals to navigate moral dilemmas with clarity and balance.

- **Justice (Adl):** Justice is the bedrock of social harmony and individual righteousness. In the Islamic tradition, it goes beyond the administration of laws to encompass a universal principle that ensures fairness, equity, and respect for human dignity. Al-Razi's reflections underscore that true justice is rooted in divine wisdom and manifests as a sincere commitment to balance, whether in personal relationships or in broader societal interactions.

- **Courage (Shuja'ah):** More than mere bravery, courage in Islamic ethics involves the moral fortitude to pursue truth and stand up for what is right, even in the face of adversity. This virtue is linked with both physical and spiritual resilience—a willingness to confront one's own shortcomings and the injustices of the world.
- **Temperance (Iqtisad):** Moderation in all things is a recurrent theme in Islamic thought. Temperance—or self-restraint—ensures that desires and passions are harmonized with reason and ethical purpose. It is the discipline that prevents excess and fosters a balanced lifestyle, enabling the individual to channel energy into constructive pursuits.

The Interrelation of Virtues

Islamic scholars have long emphasized that these cardinal virtues are interdependent. Wisdom informs justice, courage gives substance to the pursuit of truth, and temperance provides the self-control needed to act justly and wisely. This interrelation reflects a holistic view of the human being, where ethical virtues are not isolated traits but a harmonious network that supports both individual fulfillment and societal well-being. In this vision, cultivating one virtue naturally strengthens others, creating a resilient moral character that mirrors the divine attributes.

The Role of Virtues in the Spiritual Journey

For al-Razi and his contemporaries, virtues are also the means through which the soul ascends toward spiritual perfection. Each virtuous act is seen as a step on the journey to closeness with the Divine—a process that transforms the self from within. The cultivation of virtues is both an individual responsibility and a communal endeavor, where personal excellence contributes to the moral uplift of society. The cardinal virtues, therefore, are not only standards for conduct; they are also markers of spiritual progress and reflections of a deeper, transcendent truth.

Strategies for Moral Improvement

The Process of Self-Examination

The journey toward moral excellence begins with self-examination—a rigorous and honest assessment of one's habits, thoughts, and behaviors. Al-Razi advocates for a reflective practice wherein the individual constantly evaluates their actions against the backdrop of divine principles. This self-examination is not an exercise in self-criticism but a constructive process that identifies areas for growth and renewal. Techniques such as regular introspection, journaling of one's moral progress, and seeking counsel from trusted mentors are essential tools in this ongoing process.

Education and Intellectual Cultivation

Moral improvement is inextricably linked with the pursuit of knowledge. In the Islamic tradition, education is revered not only as an intellectual pursuit but also as a means of moral formation. Al-Razi emphasizes that true education nurtures both the mind and the heart. Studying classical texts, engaging in philosophical debates, and reflecting on the teachings of the Quran and the Prophet's example serve to elevate one's understanding of ethical principles. Such intellectual cultivation fosters the virtue of wisdom, enabling individuals to make informed decisions that are in harmony with the moral order.

Practicing **Mindfulness and Self-Discipline**

A KEY ASPECT of moral improvement is the development of self-discipline—a conscious effort to regulate one's desires and impulses in pursuit of higher goals. Techniques such as mindfulness, prayer, and meditation are valued practices in Islamic ethics. They not only bring inner calm and clarity but also help individuals resist the lure of immediate gratification in favor of long-term virtue. By practicing mindfulness, one becomes attuned to the subtle ways in which habits form and can intervene before negative impulses take root. This discipline is crucial for transforming potential vices into virtues through consistent, deliberate effort.

Emulating **Exemplary Figures**

IN THE RICH tapestry of Islamic history, countless exemplars of moral excellence serve as guiding lights for those seeking to improve. Al-Razi himself is celebrated not only for his intellectual prowess but also for his ethical conduct. Emulating such figures—be they classical scholars, spiritual leaders, or virtuous contemporaries—provides a practical model for behavior. The process of imitation, when undertaken with sincerity and critical reflection, can help individuals internalize the habits and dispositions that constitute true virtue. In doing so, one gradually moves from merely knowing what is right to consistently acting upon that knowledge.

Community and Accountability

Moral improvement is not a solitary journey. The role of community is paramount in shaping ethical behavior. In a supportive social environment, individuals are held accountable for their actions, and positive habits are reinforced through mutual encouragement and shared values. Communities that foster open dialogue, collective reflection, and a commitment to justice help create an atmosphere in which moral excellence can flourish. Peer support, mentoring relationships, and communal rituals of reflection provide essential structures that nurture continuous growth. Through collective accountability, the virtues become not only personal achievements but also communal treasures that elevate society as a whole.

Overcoming Vices through Reflective Practice

The path to virtue is illuminated not only by the pursuit of positive qualities but also by the active struggle against vices. Recognizing the sources of negative behavior is essential for transforming them into strengths. Al-Razi encourages a methodical approach to overcoming vices—whether they be arrogance, greed, envy, or sloth—by first acknowledging their presence, understanding their underlying causes, and then applying reason and discipline to counteract them. This reflective practice involves both introspection and external support, as individuals learn to substitute harmful habits with constructive alternatives. By systematically addressing and reforming their weaknesses, individuals pave the way for the full expression of virtuous qualities.

CONCLUSION

CHAPTER 16 HAS TRAVERSED the expansive terrain of virtues and vices—a dual framework that lies at the heart of moral and spiritual development. Through the lens of Islamic thought, and drawing heavily on the insights of al-Razi, we have examined the cardinal virtues—wisdom, justice, courage, and temperance—as the pillars upon which ethical life is built. These virtues, far from being isolated ideals, form an interconnected network that supports both individual character and the well-being of the community. They are the natural reflections of divine attributes, offering a blueprint for human excellence that is both practical and transcendent.

EQUALLY IMPORTANT, this chapter has outlined strategies for moral improvement—a comprehensive roadmap that includes self-examination, education, mindfulness, the emulation of exemplary figures, and the nurturing power of community. These strategies offer a dynamic approach to overcoming vices and cultivating virtues, enabling individuals to transform their lives in pursuit of moral perfection.

IN EMBRACING THESE TEACHINGS, we are reminded that the journey toward virtue is a lifelong endeavor—one that requires continuous reflection, disciplined practice, and the courage to change. It is a process that not only refines the individual soul but also contributes to the collective moral fabric of society, reflecting the eternal quest for goodness that is at the very core of human existence.

17
THE IDEAL HUMAN BEING

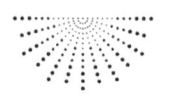

In this chapter, we explore one of the most ambitious and inspiring ideals in Islamic thought—the concept of the ideal human being. This ideal is not simply an abstract notion, but rather a concrete and attainable model of excellence that shapes ethical behavior, spiritual aspiration, and intellectual achievement. Drawing upon a rich tapestry of theological insights and philosophical reflections, al-Razi and other scholars have long considered the perfect man—or *al-Insan al-Kamil*—as the embodiment of divine attributes. At the same time, the lives of prophets and saints offer living examples of this ideal, guiding believers on the path toward moral and spiritual perfection.

The Concept of the Perfect Man (al-Insan al-Kamil)

Defining the Ideal

The notion of *al-Insan al-Kamil*, or the Perfect Man, occupies a central position in Islamic philosophy and mysticism. This concept is not about achieving flawlessness in every worldly aspect, but rather about realizing a state in which the human being becomes a complete reflection of the divine qualities. For al-Razi, the Perfect Man is a microcosm of the universe—a being whose inner and outer dimensions are perfectly aligned with the natural order and the immutable attributes of God. In this state, the individual exhibits the highest levels of wisdom, justice, and compassion, acting as a living testament to the potential embedded within the human soul.

The Journey Toward Perfection

Attaining the status of *al-Insan al-Kamil* is seen as the ultimate goal of human development—a lifelong process of self-purification and refinement. This journey requires the integration of intellectual, moral, and spiritual practices. The seeker must engage in rigorous self-examination, cultivate knowledge through both rational inquiry and divine revelation, and strive to embody virtues that elevate the soul. The process is not instantaneous; it involves enduring hardships, learning from failures, and constantly reorienting oneself toward truth and goodness.

Characteristics of the Perfect Man

In al-Razi's vision, the Perfect Man is marked by several defining characteristics:

- **Spiritual Illumination:** The ideal is illuminated by

divine light. This illumination is not merely an intellectual understanding but a deep, experiential awareness of the presence of God, which transforms the individual from within.

- **Moral Rectitude:** The Perfect Man is committed to justice, compassion, and integrity. Every action, whether in personal relationships or in the broader social context, reflects an unwavering adherence to ethical principles.
- **Intellectual Mastery:** Possessing a refined intellect, the ideal human is capable of critical thought and deep reflection. This intellectual prowess is harmonized with humility and a continuous desire for knowledge.
- **Emotional Balance:** Emotions are acknowledged as vital to human experience, yet they are regulated by reason and guided by higher moral standards. The perfect being experiences passion without being overwhelmed by it, ensuring that feelings serve rather than subjugate reason.
- **Integration of Body and Soul:** The concept of perfection in human nature includes the harmonious development of both the material and immaterial aspects. The physical body is cared for as the vessel of spiritual expression, while the soul is nurtured through practices that enhance inner clarity and moral vision.

THE PERFECT MAN as a Model of Universal Harmony

THE IDEA of *al-Insan al-Kamil* goes beyond individual attainment. It is also a model for social and cosmic harmony. When a person reaches a state of perfection, they not only transform themselves but also contribute to the order and well-being of society. In Islamic thought, the Perfect Man is seen as the intermediary between the divine and the created order—a channel through which the attributes of God are manifested in the world. By embodying the highest virtues, this individual helps restore balance, heal divisions, and inspire collective progress.

Philosophical and Theological Dimensions

Al-Razi's discourse on the Perfect Man is imbued with both philosophical and theological significance. Philosophically, the ideal human represents the culmination of intellectual and moral development. It is the endpoint of a journey of self-discovery where one transcends the limitations of finite existence and attains a form of wisdom that mirrors the eternal. Theologically, *al-Insan al-Kamil* is a reflection of God's creative power. It serves as evidence that human beings, created in the image of the Divine, have the potential to actualize that image in their lives. This belief reinforces the idea that every human being carries within them a spark of the divine, and that by nurturing this spark, one can contribute to the unfolding of a greater cosmic purpose.

The Role of Prophets and Saints

Exemplars of Divine Perfection

Within the Islamic tradition, the lives of prophets and saints serve as the most vivid illustrations of *al-Insan al-Kamil*. These individuals are revered not merely for their extraordinary piety, but for the way in which their lives encapsulate the highest moral, intellectual, and spiritual ideals. Prophets, by virtue of their direct connection to divine revelation, embody a perfection that is both inspirational and instructive. They articulate the divine message in a manner that is accessible yet profoundly transformative, guiding their communities toward a greater understanding of truth and justice.

Prophets as Models of Moral and Intellectual Excellence

The prophets occupy a unique place in the ethical and spiritual landscape. They are tasked with conveying God's will, serving as conduits between the Creator and creation. Their lives are replete with examples of sacrifice, steadfastness in the face of adversity, and an unwavering commitment to moral rectitude. For instance, the life of Prophet Muhammad is seen as the quintessence of ethical conduct, combining compassion, wisdom, and resilience. His example sets a benchmark against which all human actions can be measured, demonstrating that true excellence is achieved when one aligns personal will with divine guidance.

Moreover, prophets are not solely moral exemplars; they are also intellectual innovators. They challenge prevailing norms, introduce new paradigms of thought, and encourage critical engagement with both tradition and contemporary realities. In this way, prophets serve as catalysts for intellectual and social renewal, prompting individuals to rise above mundane concerns and strive for a more enlightened existence.

Saints as Living Manifestations of the Ideal

. . .

COMPLEMENTING the role of prophets are the saints—individuals who, through their exemplary lives, embody the possibility of attaining *al-Insan al-Kamil*. Saints are often regarded as living symbols of divine grace and moral fortitude. Their lives are characterized by extraordinary acts of charity, profound spiritual insight, and a relentless commitment to truth. The veneration of saints in Islamic culture reflects a deep-seated belief that human beings can, through disciplined practice and sincere devotion, transcend their inherent limitations and achieve a state of sublime perfection.

SAINTS PROVIDE accessible role models for the faithful, demonstrating that the pursuit of virtue is not reserved for an elite few but is open to all who dedicate themselves to the path of self-improvement. Their stories serve as a source of inspiration and guidance, illustrating the transformative power of faith, perseverance, and compassion. Whether through miraculous acts, sustained periods of asceticism, or everyday examples of selfless service, saints exemplify the practical application of the principles embodied in the concept of the Perfect Man.

THE INTERPLAY Between Prophetic Guidance and Personal Effort

A KEY ASPECT of the ideal human being is the dynamic interplay between prophetic guidance and individual striving. While prophets and saints provide the blueprint for what is possible, the realization of *al-Insan al-Kamil* ultimately depends on personal effort and commitment. Islamic thought emphasizes that every individual is responsible for cultivating their own inner potential. The prophetic tradition offers not a prescription for automatic perfection but a call to actively engage in the process of self-transformation. In this sense, the lives of prophets and saints serve as both inspiration and challenge—urging each person to embrace the rigorous journey of moral and intellectual refinement.

The Role of Community in Fostering the Ideal

THE COLLECTIVE DIMENSION of ethical life is also critical in realizing the ideal human being. Prophets and saints are not isolated figures; they function within communities that both nurture and are transformed by their presence. In an ideal society, the pursuit of moral and intellectual excellence is a shared endeavor. The teachings of prophets provide the foundation for communal ethics, while the examples of saints help to cultivate a culture of compassion, justice, and mutual support. Together, they foster an environment in which the pursuit of *al-Insan al-Kamil* becomes not just an individual aspiration but a collective mission—a way for society to elevate itself by aspiring to the highest standards of virtue.

Conclusion

CHAPTER 17 HAS TAKEN us on a rich exploration of the ideal human being—the vision of *al-Insan al-Kamil*—as articulated in Islamic thought and exemplified by prophets and saints. We have seen that the Perfect Man is far more than an abstract ideal; it is a living model of how human beings can reflect divine attributes through the harmonious integration of moral, intellectual, and spiritual excellence. This vision challenges us to embark on a lifelong journey of self-improvement—a journey that involves rigorous self-examination, the cultivation of wisdom and virtue, and the conscious effort to align our lives with the eternal principles that govern the universe.

The exemplary lives of prophets and saints serve as beacons on this journey, illustrating both the possibility and the profound benefits of attaining a state of perfection. They remind us that while the ideal may seem distant, it is a reality that each individual can strive toward through dedication, compassion, and unwavering commitment to truth. In this dynamic interplay between divine inspiration and personal effort, we find a model for living that not only transforms the self but also contributes to the moral and spiritual uplift of the community as a whole.

Ultimately, the concept of the ideal human being invites us to view our lives as a continuous process of growth and refinement—a process in which every act of kindness, every moment of insight, and every step toward ethical clarity brings us closer to realizing our highest potential. In embracing this vision, we honor the divine spark within us and participate in the unfolding of a grand, cosmic narrative —one that celebrates the eternal quest for excellence and the profound dignity of the human soul.

18
PRINCIPLES OF QUR'ANIC INTERPRETATION

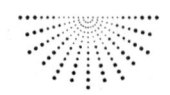

This chapter delves into one of the most complex and vital areas of Islamic intellectual tradition: the interpretation of the Qur'an. Through a careful analysis of literal and allegorical approaches, along with the crucial role of reason in exegesis—as articulated in works like *Mafatih al-Ghayb*—we explore the diverse methods used to unlock the layered meanings of the sacred text. This investigation not only illuminates the multifaceted nature of Qur'anic interpretation but also underscores its relevance as a dynamic dialogue between revelation and human intellect.

Literal vs. Allegorical **Interpretation**

The Literal Approach: **Grounding in the Text**

The literal interpretation of the Qur'an seeks to understand its verses according to the plain meaning of the words and phrases as they are conventionally used. This method emphasizes:

- **Clarity and Precision:** Proponents argue that the Qur'an is revealed in clear, unambiguous language. By adhering to the apparent meanings of the words, interpreters preserve the text's original message without imposing subjective interpretations.
- **Historical and Linguistic Context:** Literal exegesis involves a deep engagement with the linguistic nuances of classical Arabic and the historical context in which the Qur'an was revealed. Scholars draw on the lexicon of the language, the idiomatic expressions of the time, and the cultural milieu of early Muslim communities to ground their interpretations.
- **Preservation of the Divine Message:** For many traditionalists, a literal reading is seen as a safeguard against human distortions. It is believed that the Qur'an, as the word of God, is meant to be understood directly—its truths accessible to all who read it with sincerity and reverence.

However, literalism also faces challenges. Critics point out that language is inherently layered and that rigid literalism may sometimes fail to capture the full spiritual and metaphysical dimensions intended by the revelation. This is particularly evident when the text employs symbolism or metaphorical language to convey deeper truths.

The Allegorical Approach: Seeking Hidden Depths

In contrast, allegorical interpretation goes beyond the apparent meanings to uncover the inner, often symbolic, dimensions of the Qur'anic text. This method:

- **Reveals Multiple Layers of Meaning:** Allegorical exegesis posits that the Qur'an speaks on several levels simultaneously—a surface level that addresses immediate, practical concerns and a deeper level that explores metaphysical and existential truths.
- **Emphasizes Spiritual and Ethical Lessons:** Many verses of the Qur'an, when read allegorically, provide timeless lessons on morality, spirituality, and the nature of existence. Allegorists suggest that the symbolic language of the Qur'an is intended to inspire and transform the heart, encouraging believers to reflect on the ultimate realities of life.
- **Accommodates Diversity of Thought:** The allegorical method acknowledges the variability of human experience and the limitations of literal language in conveying the ineffable. By embracing metaphor, allegorists offer interpretations that can resonate with diverse audiences, addressing both the mind and the soul.

Despite its profound potential, the allegorical approach carries risks. It may lead to excessive subjectivism if personal or cultural biases overwhelm the interpretative process. Al-Razi and other scholars, therefore, caution that allegory should be employed in a disciplined manner, always anchored in the broader context of Islamic theology and tradition.

Harmonizing Literal and Allegorical Readings

The most compelling interpretations of the Qur'an often emerge from a balanced synthesis of both literal and allegorical methods. Such a balanced approach recognizes that while the literal meaning provides a necessary foundation, the allegorical interpretation enriches the understanding by opening avenues to deeper, often hidden, insights. This dual method:

- **Respects the Integrity of the Text:** By acknowledging the plain meaning of the words while simultaneously exploring their symbolic resonance, interpreters can capture the multifaceted nature of divine revelation.
- **Encourages Intellectual Humility:** Recognizing the limitations of any single interpretative method, scholars remain open to multiple perspectives and ongoing refinement of understanding.
- **Fosters a Dynamic Dialogue:** The interplay between literal and allegorical exegesis mirrors the dynamic interaction between revelation and reason—a central theme in Islamic thought.

The Role of Reason in Exegesis (Mafatih al-Ghayb)

Rational Inquiry as a Tool for Understanding

Al-Razi's approach to Qur'anic interpretation is characterized by a firm belief in the power of reason to unlock divine mysteries. In works such as *Mafatih al-Ghayb*, he articulates the view that human intellect is not antithetical to revelation but rather a crucial instrument in its comprehension. This perspective is founded on several key principles:

- **Systematic Analysis:** Reason enables scholars to examine the structure, language, and context of the Qur'anic text systematically. Through logical analysis and critical

inquiry, interpreters can resolve apparent contradictions and identify recurring themes.
- **Integration of Diverse Disciplines:** The use of reason in exegesis is enriched by insights from linguistics, philosophy, theology, and even natural sciences. This interdisciplinary approach allows for a more comprehensive understanding of the text, situating it within a broader intellectual framework.
- **The Pursuit of Truth:** For al-Razi, reason is a manifestation of the divine gift of intellect. It is a means by which humans can ascend from the mundane to the sublime, gradually uncovering the layers of meaning embedded in the revelation. Reason, when applied with sincerity and rigor, becomes a tool for both personal transformation and communal enlightenment.

The Limits and Possibilities of Rational Exegesis

While reason is invaluable, al-Razi also recognizes its limitations. The divine nature of the Qur'an means that certain aspects of the text may transcend purely rational explanation. In these instances:
- **The Complementarity of Revelation:** Reason must work in tandem with revelation. The insights gleaned from the text itself, as well as from the broader Islamic tradition, serve as a corrective to overly mechanistic or reductive readings.
- **Maintaining a Balance:** Excessive reliance on rationalism may lead to interpretations that are detached from the spiritual and ethical core of the Qur'an. Therefore, a balanced approach respects both the intellectual and the mystical dimensions of the text.
- **Openness to Mystery:** The acknowledgment of the

limits of human reason invites an attitude of humility. The Qur'an, in its infinite wisdom, contains mysteries that may never be fully unraveled. This recognition does not diminish the value of rational inquiry; rather, it situates it within a broader quest for meaning that is as much about embracing uncertainty as it is about discovering clarity.

The Legacy of Mafatih al-Ghayb

MAFATIH AL-GHAYB STANDS as a testament to the rich tradition of Qur'anic exegesis that harmonizes reason with revelation. In this work, al-Razi not only provides detailed commentary on the literal meanings of the verses but also delves into their allegorical dimensions, using reason as a guiding principle. His method involves:

- **Rigorous Textual Analysis:** Drawing on classical Arabic grammar and literary criticism to elucidate the nuances of the text.
- **Philosophical Reflection:** Engaging with metaphysical questions and ethical dilemmas raised by the Qur'anic verses, thereby linking the text to broader questions about the nature of existence.
- **Integrative Synthesis:** Offering interpretations that honor both the explicit and implicit dimensions of the Qur'an, ensuring that the exegesis remains faithful to the spirit of the revelation while also engaging contemporary intellectual challenges.

By placing reason at the heart of exegesis, al-Razi demonstrates that the Qur'an is not a static document but a living text—one that continues to speak to each generation in fresh and meaningful ways. His approach underscores the idea that the pursuit of knowledge and wisdom is an ongoing dialogue between the divine and the human, a conversation that evolves as our understanding deepens and our perspectives broaden.

CONCLUSION

CHAPTER 18 HAS OFFERED a comprehensive exploration of the principles of Qur'anic interpretation, emphasizing the interplay between literal and allegorical readings and the indispensable role of reason in the exegesis process. In understanding the Qur'an, a balanced approach that respects both the straightforward and the symbolic dimensions of the text provides a richer, more nuanced vision of divine revelation. The insights of al-Razi, as illuminated in *Mafatih al-Ghayb*, remind us that the Qur'an is a multi-layered tapestry —one that invites us to engage our intellect and our spirit in an ever-evolving quest for truth.

THIS CHAPTER not only celebrates the intellectual rigor of classical exegesis but also encourages modern readers to approach the sacred text with both reverence and critical inquiry. Through this dynamic engagement, the Qur'an continues to inspire, challenge, and elevate the human soul, guiding believers toward a deeper understanding of themselves, their faith, and the boundless mysteries of existence.

19

KEY THEMES IN AL-RAZI'S COMMENTARY

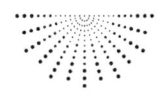

In this chapter, we delve into the intellectual tapestry woven by al-Razi in his Qur'anic commentary, examining the key themes that run through his exegeses. His work not only illuminates the profound meanings embedded in the sacred text but also engages in a critical dialogue with earlier commentaries. By selecting important verses and exploring al-Razi's interpretations, we uncover his innovative synthesis of reason, revelation, and tradition. Furthermore, we examine how he both respects and critiques the contributions of previous commentators, establishing a distinctive methodological framework that has influenced generations of Islamic scholarship.

Selected **Exegeses of Important Verses**

Illuminating **the Nature of Divine Revelation**

. . .

ONE OF THE recurring themes in al-Razi's exegesis is the nuanced understanding of divine revelation. In his commentary, he often underscores the layered nature of Qur'anic language. For instance, when examining verses that describe the light of God or the illumination of truth, al-Razi emphasizes that these images are not solely literal depictions of brightness but metaphors for the multifaceted process of acquiring knowledge and spiritual insight. He argues that the divine light represents the interplay of rational inquiry and mystical experience—a dual source of enlightenment that empowers the soul to transcend its limited, worldly perspective.

The Role of Reason and the Unfolding of Moral Order

ANOTHER KEY THEME in al-Razi's commentary is his insistence on the harmonious relationship between reason and revelation. In selected exegeses of verses dealing with the moral and ethical injunctions of the Qur'an, he elucidates how rational deliberation is indispensable in discerning the ethical imperatives embedded in the text. For example, when interpreting verses related to justice and the treatment of others, al-Razi does not restrict himself to a superficial reading; he delves into the underlying principles of moral responsibility. He contends that the Qur'anic command to act justly is both a reflection of divine wisdom and a call for individuals to engage in critical self-examination. His exegesis reveals that moral order is not imposed externally but emerges through the dynamic process of intellectual and ethical cultivation.

Addressing the Paradox of Fate and Free Will

. . .

AL-RAZI'S TREATMENT of verses discussing fate and free will is illustrative of his broader commitment to reconciling apparent contradictions within the Qur'anic narrative. In his commentary on passages that address predestination and human agency, he navigates the delicate balance between divine decree and individual autonomy. Al-Razi argues that while the cosmic order is preordained by divine wisdom, the human capacity for choice remains a vital element in the unfolding of destiny. His exegesis of these verses emphasizes that true freedom is not the absence of fate, but the ability to align one's actions with the divine order. In doing so, he offers a sophisticated framework that mitigates the tension between determinism and free will, providing believers with both hope and accountability.

The Symbolism of the Natural World

AL-RAZI FREQUENTLY EMPLOYS the natural world as a mirror for understanding metaphysical truths. When interpreting verses that refer to the beauty, order, and regularity of creation, he elucidates how nature itself is a testament to the unity and coherence of divine revelation. He interprets the cyclical patterns in nature—not only as evidence of natural laws but also as allegories for spiritual cycles of death, renewal, and ascension. For instance, a verse that speaks of the alternation of night and day is seen as symbolizing the continuous struggle between ignorance and enlightenment— a reminder that the human journey toward knowledge is iterative and progressive.

. . .

Integration of Empirical Observation with Metaphysical Inquiry

Al-Razi's exegeses often bridge the gap between empirical observation and metaphysical speculation. When he encounters verses that hint at natural phenomena—be it the expansion of the universe or the intricate processes underlying creation—he draws on his familiarity with contemporary scientific thought. His interpretations reflect an early attempt to integrate empirical insights with spiritual truths. In doing so, al-Razi not only enriches the exegesis with practical examples from the natural world but also reaffirms the notion that the study of the universe is itself an act of worship, a way of understanding the divine order that underpins all existence.

Al-Razi's Engagement with Previous Commentators

Respect for Traditional Exegesis

Al-Razi's commentary is deeply rooted in the classical tradition of Qur'anic exegesis. He often acknowledges the contributions of earlier commentators—such as al-Tabari, al-Zamakhshari, and others—recognizing that their works have laid the foundational framework for understanding the sacred text. In many instances, he quotes and refers to their interpretations, using them as starting points for further exploration. This respect for tradition reflects his broader belief in the cumulative nature of knowledge, where each generation builds upon the insights of its predecessors.

. . .

Critical Reappraisal and Refinement

While al-Razi shows reverence for earlier scholarship, he is equally unafraid to offer critical reappraisals of traditional interpretations. In his exegesis, he often identifies areas where he believes previous commentators have either oversimplified complex ideas or failed to reconcile conflicting interpretations. For example, in discussing the allegorical dimensions of certain verses, al-Razi critiques those who adhere strictly to literalism. He argues that such an approach can obscure the deeper, symbolic meanings that are essential for a comprehensive understanding of the text. His critical stance is not meant to dismiss earlier interpretations outright but to refine and enhance them, advocating for a more balanced approach that respects both the apparent and hidden dimensions of revelation.

Methodological Innovations

Al-Razi's engagement with previous commentators is also characterized by methodological innovation. He introduces a more systematic use of reason in exegesis, insisting that intellectual inquiry should accompany traditional methods. By employing a dialectical method, he weaves together various strands of interpretation—literal, allegorical, ethical, and scientific—into a coherent narrative that transcends the limitations of any single approach. His methodology reflects a desire to harmonize the insights of tradition with the demands of contemporary intellectual rigor. This integrative approach has had a lasting impact on subsequent generations of scholars, who continue to draw upon al-Razi's balanced synthesis in their own interpretative work.

. . .

The Dialogue Between Revelation and Reason

At the heart of al-Razi's engagement with previous commentators is a profound dialogue between revelation and reason. He contends that neither domain can claim absolute authority over the other; instead, they must operate in a synergistic relationship that enriches both. This view is particularly evident in his treatment of ambiguous verses, where he invites multiple interpretations that accommodate both the clear, expository elements of the text and its more mysterious, symbolic aspects. In doing so, al-Razi encourages an interpretative flexibility that remains faithful to the spirit of the Qur'an while also adapting to the evolving landscape of human knowledge.

The Legacy of Critical Engagement

The legacy of al-Razi's engagement with earlier commentators is one of critical reflection and continuous intellectual evolution. His work demonstrates that the Qur'anic text is not a static artifact but a living document whose meanings unfold through ongoing dialogue and reinterpretation. By acknowledging the strengths and limitations of previous interpretations, al-Razi sets a standard for scholarly inquiry that is both respectful of tradition and open to innovation. His approach has inspired countless scholars to explore the Qur'an with fresh eyes, always mindful of the need to balance inherited wisdom with the insights gleaned from personal reflection and contemporary thought.

. . .

Conclusion

CHAPTER 19 HAS PROVIDED a comprehensive examination of the key themes in al-Razi's Qur'anic commentary. Through selected exegeses of important verses, we have seen how he delves into the nature of divine revelation, the interplay between reason and symbolism, and the moral and metaphysical dimensions of the text. His interpretations reveal a profound commitment to a balanced understanding—one that embraces both the literal and allegorical meanings embedded in the Qur'anic narrative.

FURTHERMORE, al-Razi's engagement with previous commentators underscores his dedication to building upon the rich heritage of Islamic scholarship while also challenging and refining it. His respectful yet critical dialogue with earlier interpretations highlights the dynamic and evolving nature of exegesis, where every generation is called to reexamine and deepen its understanding of divine wisdom.

IN SUM, al-Razi's commentary stands as a testament to the enduring power of thoughtful, integrative interpretation—a process that not only elucidates the mysteries of the Qur'an but also inspires a continuous quest for knowledge, ethical clarity, and spiritual growth. Through his work, we are reminded that the journey of understanding is as infinite and multifaceted as the divine revelation itself, inviting us to explore, question, and ultimately, to be transformed by the profound insights contained within the sacred text.

20
REVELATION AND PHILOSOPHY

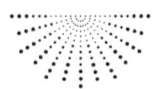

In this culminating chapter, we explore the profound interplay between revelation and philosophy—a dialogue that lies at the heart of Islamic intellectual tradition. Al-Razi, among other great scholars, navigated the delicate balance between the divine illumination of revelation and the rigorous demands of reason. His work provides us with a roadmap for understanding how these two sources of knowledge can be harmonized, even as human intellect remains inevitably bounded by its own limitations.

Harmonizing Reason and Revelation

A Dual Source of Enlightenment

At the core of al-Razi's thought is the belief that revelation and reason are not adversaries, but rather complementary sources of truth. Revelation, transmitted through sacred texts and prophetic tradition, offers insights into the transcendent and eternal aspects of existence. It speaks to the soul's innermost yearnings and to the moral imperatives that guide human behavior. Meanwhile, reason—our innate intellectual faculty—enables us to examine, interpret, and contextualize these divine messages within the framework of the observable world. Together, they provide a dual source of enlightenment, where the poetic and the logical converge to reveal a deeper understanding of reality.

The Role of Exegesis in Synthesis

For al-Razi, the process of exegesis is a key means of achieving this synthesis. Through careful interpretation of the Qur'anic text and other divine revelations, he demonstrated how rational analysis could elucidate the hidden layers of meaning within the sacred words. His commentary often reveals that what appears on the surface as simple or literal may, in fact, be imbued with allegorical and philosophical significance. This dual reading—acknowledging both the manifest and the hidden dimensions—exemplifies how reason can work in tandem with revelation. It allows for a dynamic understanding that is continually refined through both empirical observation and spiritual insight.

The Dynamic Interplay of Mind and Spirit

Al-Razi's approach is characterized by an ongoing dialogue between the rational mind and the receptive heart. He contended that neither domain should be subordinated to the other. Instead, a mature intellectual life is one in which reason is enriched by the insights of revelation, while the spiritual quest is grounded in critical thought. This dynamic interplay encourages a form of intellectual humility, where even the most profound insights are open to reevaluation and deeper understanding. By embracing both dimensions, al-Razi invites us to see truth not as a static end-product but as an evolving process—one that continually expands the horizons of human understanding.

Addressing Controversies and Misconceptions

Throughout his works, al-Razi was keenly aware of the controversies that arise when reason and revelation seem to conflict. Critics often argued that rational inquiry could undermine the authority of divine revelation, while others feared that a purely literalist approach would stifle intellectual growth. Al-Razi navigated these challenges by proposing that apparent contradictions are often the result of a limited perspective. When reason and revelation are allowed to speak to each other freely, they can resolve their differences in ways that enrich both. His balanced methodology offers a way to honor the sanctity of divine insight without sacrificing the critical clarity that reason provides.

The Limits of Human Understanding

Recognizing the Boundaries of the Finite Mind

Despite the power of reason and the transformative potential of revelation, al-Razi was acutely aware that human understanding is inherently limited. Our finite minds, shaped by time and space, can only grasp so much of the infinite and the eternal. This recognition of our cognitive limitations is not a cause for despair; rather, it is a call to intellectual humility. Al-Razi maintained that while reason can pierce many veils of mystery, there will always remain elements of the divine that elude complete comprehension. This gap is not a deficiency but a reminder of the transcendent nature of ultimate truth.

The Mystery of the Divine

The limits of human understanding serve as a boundary between the knowable and the unknowable. In al-Razi's view, the mysteries of existence—such as the nature of the divine essence or the ultimate purpose of creation—are aspects of reality that may forever remain beyond the full grasp of human intellect. Revelation, then, acts as a bridge across this gap. It provides glimpses into the infinite, offering insights that, while not exhaustive, guide the soul toward a deeper engagement with the mysteries of life. The interplay of reason and revelation teaches us to appreciate that some questions may never have definitive answers, and that the journey of seeking truth is as important as any final resolution.

Embracing Intellectual Humility

One of the most profound lessons from al-Razi's philosophy is the cultivation of intellectual humility. Recognizing the limits of human understanding compels us to remain open, inquisitive, and continuously reflective. It encourages us to approach both philosophical inquiry and spiritual reflection as ongoing processes, where every answer raises new questions. In this spirit, intellectual humility becomes not a sign of weakness, but a strength that fosters continual growth. It invites us to be learners for life—ever willing to revise our assumptions and to seek a more expansive view of reality.

THE CONTINUING QUEST for Truth

IN ACKNOWLEDGING the boundaries of what can be known, al-Razi did not advocate for a retreat into skepticism or resignation. Instead, he saw these limits as an invitation to further exploration—a challenge to continually push the edges of our understanding. The very act of seeking, questioning, and striving for knowledge is, in itself, a noble pursuit. It reflects the divine impulse within us to reach beyond our immediate grasp and to connect with the greater mysteries of existence. Even as we accept the limits of our intellect, the quest for truth remains a vibrant, dynamic journey that propels us forward.

CONCLUSION

CHAPTER 20 HAS TAKEN us to the confluence of revelation and philosophy, where the luminous insights of divine revelation meet the rigorous inquiries of human reason. Al-Razi's work stands as a testament to the possibility of harmonizing these two seemingly disparate domains. By engaging in a balanced dialogue—where the literal and allegorical, the rational and the mystical, the known and the unknowable all contribute to a richer tapestry of understanding—we find that truth is a living, evolving process.

While human understanding may always be bounded by the limitations of our finite minds, the interplay between reason and revelation invites us to continually strive for a deeper, more holistic grasp of reality. In this ongoing quest, intellectual humility and a commitment to critical inquiry serve as our guiding lights. As we journey through the complexities of existence, al-Razi's vision reminds us that the pursuit of wisdom is not a final destination but an eternal endeavor—a dynamic conversation between the divine and the human, a dialogue that enriches both our intellect and our spirit.

EPILOGUE

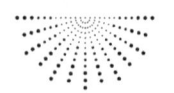

As we draw the final lines of *The Infinite Tapestry: A Masterpiece of Theology, Philosophy, and Cosmology*, a quiet reflection envelops the mind—a moment of pause in the ceaseless journey of inquiry and discovery. The pages that have come before have led us through a labyrinth of ideas, each chapter a thread woven into the vast, intricate fabric of human thought and divine mystery. Here, in this concluding meditation, we are invited to step back and contemplate the grand narrative that has unfolded—a narrative that speaks to the eternal interplay of reason and revelation, the cosmic dance of fate and free will, and the inexhaustible quest for knowledge that defines our very existence.

In the course of our journey, we have traversed landscapes of timeless wisdom, from the intricate structures of the universe to the inner sanctums of the soul. We have questioned the nature of time and space, explored the delicate balance between the material and the immaterial, and examined the profound implications of moral responsibility and divine justice. Each theme, each insight, has served as a beacon, guiding us through the maze of human experience and pointing toward the infinite—a reminder that the search for truth is an ever-unfolding process, as boundless as the cosmos itself.

THROUGHOUT THESE CHAPTERS, the voice of al-Razi resonates —a voice that calls for a harmonious blending of intellect and faith, urging us to look beyond the immediate and the superficial, to seek instead the deeper currents that shape our lives. His commentary has been our compass, challenging us to embrace both the clarity of rational inquiry and the mystery of divine revelation. In the interplay between literal meanings and allegorical depths, between the tangible evidence of the natural world and the ineffable beauty of the spiritual realm, we have come to appreciate that truth is not a static destination but a dynamic, ever-evolving journey.

NOW, as the final notes of this work echo in our hearts, we are left with a profound sense of wonder—a recognition that every ending is but the prelude to a new beginning. The insights gained here are not final answers; they are invitations to continue the dialogue, to persist in the quest for understanding even as we acknowledge the inherent limits of our finite minds. Our exploration has shown us that while the mysteries of existence may never be fully unraveled, the pursuit of wisdom enriches our lives in immeasurable ways. It is through questioning, through persistent inquiry and humble reflection, that we draw closer to the divine, transforming our perceptions and deepening our connection with the cosmos.

. . .

IN THIS SPIRIT of eternal pursuit, the epilogue does not serve as a conclusion in the traditional sense, but rather as an open door—an invitation to carry forward the legacy of this inquiry into every aspect of our lives. It encourages us to nurture the flame of curiosity, to engage with the world and its myriad wonders with both critical insight and heartfelt reverence. The tapestry we have explored together is ever-expanding, its threads interwoven with the stories of countless seekers across the ages, each contributing to the rich mosaic of human understanding.

MAY this work inspire you to continue your own journey—a journey marked by the courage to question, the humility to learn, and the determination to seek out the truth that lies hidden beneath the surface of everyday existence. As you step beyond these pages, remember that the universe is a living, vibrant testament to the interplay of the known and the mysterious; that every moment is an opportunity to glimpse the divine; and that the pursuit of knowledge is a sacred endeavor that unites us all in a timeless quest for meaning.

IN CLOSING, let this epilogue be a reminder that while our explorations here have reached a natural pause, the conversation between revelation and philosophy, between the finite and the infinite, is never truly complete. The journey continues in every thought, every act of reflection, and every heartfelt prayer for wisdom. And so, with the quiet assurance that the search for truth is as infinite as the cosmos, we bid farewell—not as an ending, but as an open invitation to discover, to wonder, and to live in the radiant light of eternal inquiry.